NORTH
AND
SOUTH
KOREA

OPPOSING VIEWPOINTS ®

Other Books of Related Interest

OPPOSING VIEWPOINTS SERIES

American Foreign Policy
The Breakup of the Soviet Union
Censorship
China
Civil Liberties
Human Rights
Russia
War
Weapons of Mass Destruction

CURRENT CONTROVERSIES SERIES

Censorship
Civil Liberties
Developing Nations
Free Speech
Nationalism and Ethnic Conflict

AT ISSUE SERIES

Missile Defense
National Security
Nuclear Security
Should There Be Limits to Free Speech?
The United Nations
U.S. Policy Toward China

NORTH AND SOUTH KOREA

OPPOSING VIEWPOINTS ®

William Dudley, *Book Editor*

Daniel Leone, *President*
Bonnie Szumski, *Publisher*
Scott Barbour, *Managing Editor*

OPPOSING
VIEWPOINTS®
SERIES

GREENHAVEN
PRESS®

THOMSON
—————*—————™
GALE

San Diego • Detroit • New York • San Francisco • Cleveland
New Haven, Conn. • Waterville, Maine • London • Munich

THOMSON

✴ ™

GALE

LIBRARY OF CONGRESS CATALOGING-IN-PUBLICATION DATA

Dudley, William, 1964–
  North and South Korea / William Dudley, book editor.
    p. cm. — (Opposing viewpoints)
  Includes bibliographical references and index.
  ISBN 0-7377-1235-X (pbk. : alk. paper) —
  ISBN 0-7377-1236-8 (hardback : alk. paper)
    1. United States—Foreign relations—Korea (North). 2. Korea (North)—Foreign relations—United States. 3. United States—Military relations—Korea (South). 4. Korea (South)—Military relations—United States. [1. United States—Foreign relations—Korea. 2. Korea—Foreign relations—United States. 3. Korea (North)—Politics and government—1960– . 4. Korea (South)—Politics and government—1960–]. I. Title. II. Series.
E183.8.K7 D84 2003
x—dc21
                                                    2002000497

Printed in the United States of America

"Congress shall make no law...abridging the freedom of speech, or of the press."

First Amendment to the U.S. Constitution

The basic foundation of our democracy is the First Amendment guarantee of freedom of expression. The Opposing Viewpoints Series is dedicated to the concept of this basic freedom and the idea that it is more important to practice it than to enshrine it.

Contents

Why Consider Opposing Viewpoints?   9

Introduction   12

Chapter 1: Is North Korea a Serious Threat?

Chapter Preface   18

1. North Korea Is a Serious Military Threat   19
   U.S. Department of Defense

2. North Korea's Military Threat Has Been
   Exaggerated   26
   John M. Swomley

3. A Missile Defense System Is Needed Against
   North Korea   34
   Paul Wolfowitz

4. A Missile Defense System Is Not Needed
   Against North Korea   39
   Leon V. Sigal

Periodical Bibliography   43

**Chapter 2: What Is the State of Democracy and
   Human Rights in North and South Korea?**

Chapter Preface   45

1. South Korea Has Achieved Democracy   47
   Larry Diamond and Doh Chull Shin

2. South Korea Has Not Yet Achieved Democracy   55
   John Kie-chiang Oh

3. North Korea's Government Has Served Its
   People Well   64
   Hugh Stephens

4. North Korea's Government Has Severely
   Oppressed Its People   74
   International Human Rights League of Korea

Periodical Bibliography   85

> "Congress shall make no law. . . abridging the freedom of speech, or of the press."

First Amendment to the U.S. Constitution

The basic foundation of our democracy is the First Amendment guarantee of freedom of expression. The Opposing Viewpoints Series is dedicated to the concept of this basic freedom and the idea that it is more important to practice it than to enshrine it.

Contents

Why Consider Opposing Viewpoints? 9

Introduction 12

Chapter 1: Is North Korea a Serious Threat?

Chapter Preface 18

1. North Korea Is a Serious Military Threat 19
   U.S. Department of Defense

2. North Korea's Military Threat Has Been
   Exaggerated 26
   John M. Swomley

3. A Missile Defense System Is Needed Against
   North Korea 34
   Paul Wolfowitz

4. A Missile Defense System Is Not Needed
   Against North Korea 39
   Leon V. Sigal

Periodical Bibliography 43

**Chapter 2: What Is the State of Democracy and
   Human Rights in North and South Korea?**

Chapter Preface 45

1. South Korea Has Achieved Democracy 47
   Larry Diamond and Doh Chull Shin

2. South Korea Has Not Yet Achieved Democracy 55
   John Kie-chiang Oh

3. North Korea's Government Has Served Its
   People Well 64
   Hugh Stephens

4. North Korea's Government Has Severely
   Oppressed Its People 74
   International Human Rights League of Korea

Periodical Bibliography 85

Chapter 3: What Should U.S. Foreign Policy Be Toward North and South Korea?

Chapter Preface   87

1. The United States Should Withdraw from South Korea   89
   Doug Bandow

2. The United States Should Not Withdraw from South Korea   94
   Glenn Baek

3. The United States Should Engage with North Korea   98
   David Wright

4. U.S. Engagement with North Korea Has Been a Failure   108
   Christopher Cox

5. The United States Should Make Peace with North Korea   113
   Indong Oh

6. The United States Should Not Make Peace with North Korea   119
   Larry M. Wortzel

Periodical Bibliography   123

Chapter 4: What Is the Future of North and South Korea?

Chapter Preface   125

1. Korean Reunification May Be Imminent   127
   Nicholas Eberstadt

2. Korean Reunification Is Not Imminent   136
   William J. Taylor

3. South Korea Should Continue to Reach Out to North Korea   144
   Kim Dae Jung

4. South Korea's Policy of Reaching Out to North Korea Must Be Reexamined   151
   JoongAng Ilbo

5. North Korea May Attempt China-Style
   Economic and Political Reforms   155
   Michael Parks and Gregory F. Treverton

6. North Korea Will Not Attempt China-Style
   Reforms   160
   Yeon Hacheong

Periodical Bibliography   165

For Further Discussion   166
Chronology   168
Organizations and Websites   175
Bibliography of Books   179
Index   182

Why Consider Opposing Viewpoints?

"The only way in which a human being can make some approach to knowing the whole of a subject is by hearing what can be said about it by persons of every variety of opinion and studying all modes in which it can be looked at by every character of mind. No wise man ever acquired his wisdom in any mode but this."

John Stuart Mill

In our media-intensive culture it is not difficult to find differing opinions. Thousands of newspapers and magazines and dozens of radio and television talk shows resound with differing points of view. The difficulty lies in deciding which opinion to agree with and which "experts" seem the most credible. The more inundated we become with differing opinions and claims, the more essential it is to hone critical reading and thinking skills to evaluate these ideas. Opposing Viewpoints books address this problem directly by presenting stimulating debates that can be used to enhance and teach these skills. The varied opinions contained in each book examine many different aspects of a single issue. While examining these conveniently edited opposing views, readers can develop critical thinking skills such as the ability to compare and contrast authors' credibility, facts, argumentation styles, use of persuasive techniques, and other stylistic tools. In short, the Opposing Viewpoints Series is an ideal way to attain the higher-level thinking and reading skills so essential in a culture of diverse and contradictory opinions.

In addition to providing a tool for critical thinking, Opposing Viewpoints books challenge readers to question their own strongly held opinions and assumptions. Most people form their opinions on the basis of upbringing, peer pressure, and personal, cultural, or professional bias. By reading carefully balanced opposing views, readers must directly confront new ideas as well as the opinions of those with whom they disagree. This is not to simplistically argue that everyone who reads opposing views will—or should—change his or her opinion. Instead, the series enhances readers' understanding of their own views by encouraging confrontation with opposing ideas. Careful examination of others' views can lead to the readers' understanding of the logical inconsistencies in their own opinions, perspective on why they hold an opinion, and the consideration of the possibility that their opinion requires further evaluation.

Evaluating Other Opinions

To ensure that this type of examination occurs, Opposing Viewpoints books present all types of opinions. Prominent spokespeople on different sides of each issue as well as well-known professionals from many disciplines challenge the reader. An additional goal of the series is to provide a forum for other, less known, or even unpopular viewpoints. The opinion of an ordinary person who has had to make the decision to cut off life support from a terminally ill relative, for example, may be just as valuable and provide just as much insight as a medical ethicist's professional opinion. The editors have two additional purposes in including these less known views. One, the editors encourage readers to respect others' opinions—even when not enhanced by professional credibility. It is only by reading or listening to and objectively evaluating others' ideas that one can determine whether they are worthy of consideration. Two, the inclusion of such viewpoints encourages the important critical thinking skill of objectively evaluating an author's credentials and bias. This evaluation will illuminate an author's reasons for taking a particular stance on an issue and will aid in readers' evaluation of the author's ideas.

It is our hope that these books will give readers a deeper understanding of the issues debated and an appreciation of the complexity of even seemingly simple issues when good and honest people disagree. This awareness is particularly important in a democratic society such as ours in which people enter into public debate to determine the common good. Those with whom one disagrees should not be regarded as enemies but rather as people whose views deserve careful examination and may shed light on one's own.

Thomas Jefferson once said that "difference of opinion leads to inquiry, and inquiry to truth." Jefferson, a broadly educated man, argued that "if a nation expects to be ignorant and free . . . it expects what never was and never will be." As individuals and as a nation, it is imperative that we consider the opinions of others and examine them with skill and discernment. The Opposing Viewpoints Series is intended to help readers achieve this goal.

David L. Bender and Bruno Leone,
Founders

Greenhaven Press anthologies primarily consist of previously published material taken from a variety of sources, including periodicals, books, scholarly journals, newspapers, government documents, and position papers from private and public organizations. These original sources are often edited for length and to ensure their accessibility for a young adult audience. The anthology editors also change the original titles of these works in order to clearly present the main thesis of each viewpoint and to explicitly indicate the opinion presented in the viewpoint. These alterations are made in consideration of both the reading and comprehension levels of a young adult audience. Every effort is made to ensure that Greenhaven Press accurately reflects the original intent of the authors included in this anthology.

Introduction

"Koreans on either side of the dividing line . . . are brothers and sisters and cousins from the same heritage, and at the same time they are bitter enemies who have been waging fierce struggles against one another for half a century."

—Don Oberdorfer, author of The Two Koreas

The Korean peninsula—an area of eighty-five thousand square miles in northeast Asia jutting from China and abutting Japan—was a unified kingdom for thirteen hundred years. For the past half century, however, it has been a land divided. Korea's partition was a product of externally imposed events, specifically the Cold War between the United States and the Soviet Union that dominated world affairs for much of the second half of the twentieth century. Although the Cold War ended with the Soviet Union's dissolution in 1991, Korea has remained divided. Numerous observers have labeled the continuing rift between North Korea and South Korea the Cold War's last remnant. That rift overshadows Korean life on both sides of the divide.

The roots of Korea's division stem from the closing days of World War II, when troops from the United States and the Soviet Union, then wartime allies, entered Korea to liberate it from Japanese occupation (Korea had been a Japanese colony since 1910). The United States occupied the southern half of the country while the Soviet Union occupied the north. However, the two occupation zones (bordered by the 38th parallel) hardened into distinct spheres of influence as the two superpowers were unable to agree on a plan to restore Korea's government. The newly formed United Nations passed a 1947 resolution calling for elections for a single government, but the Soviet Union refused to cooperate. In 1948 two governments were formed: the Soviet-backed Democratic People's Republic of Korea, with its capital in the northern city of Pyongyang, and the American-backed Republic of Korea, with Seoul as its capital. Both regimes claimed to be the legitimate government of all of Korea.

The conflict between the two Koreas reached its bitter peak in the 1950–1953 Korean War, which was both a civil war between Koreans and an international conflict involving soldiers from around the world. North Korea, armed and advised by the Soviets, invaded South Korea in 1950 in an attempt to unify the country. The United States responded by influencing the United Nations to pass a resolution authorizing a "police action" to protect South Korea; the UN force dispatched there was led by American general Douglas MacArthur and was comprised predominantly of American troops. Those forces were able to retake almost the entire Korean peninsula before Communist China intervened with its own forces. After three years of fighting, an armistice between the warring parties ended the fighting and established a cease-fire line near the original border at the 38th parallel. However, later negotiations for a peace treaty between North and South Korea failed; the two nations remain in a technical state of war.

The war proved devastating to the peninsula, with an estimated 2 to 4 million Koreans killed from war-related causes (out of an initial population of 30 million), landscapes obliterated by heavy bombing, industry and agriculture destroyed, and its people embittered and divided. The physical damage could be repaired, but the psychological fallout proved harder to overcome. The fact that Koreans "fought and killed each other" created "a foundation for real mistrust and hatred toward each other," argues Katy Oh, an analyst for the Institute for Defense Analyses. The divisions between the two nations remain pervasive and profound. Military skirmishes periodically break out along the heavily militarized border. For decades virtually no Koreans were allowed to even visit the other nation; such visits today are confined to a very few state-sponsored ceremonial occasions, leaving millions of Koreans unable to meet with relatives across the border. There is no mail or telephone service between the two Koreas, and it is against the law in both nations to listen to radio broadcasts from the other country.

The gulf between the two Koreas has been exacerbated by their differing social, economic, and political systems. Under Kim Il Sung, the dictator of North Korea until his death in

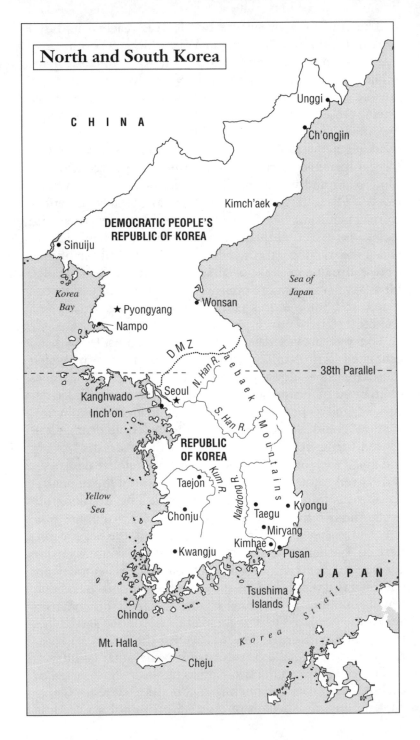

North and South Korea

CHINA

Unggi

Ch'ongjin

Kimch'aek

DEMOCRATIC PEOPLE'S
REPUBLIC OF KOREA

Sinuiju

Korea
Bay

Sea of
Japan

★ Pyongyang
Nampo

Wonsan

D M Z

N. Han R.

Taebaek

38th Parallel

Kanghwado
Inch'on

Seoul

S. Han R.

Mountains

REPUBLIC
OF KOREA

Taejon

Kum R.

Yellow
Sea

Chonju

Nakdong R.

Taegu

Kyongu

Miryang

Kwangju

Kimhae

Pusan

JAPAN

Chindo

Tsushima
Islands

Korea Strait

Mt. Halla

Cheju

1994, North Korea followed Communist models of land redistribution and collectivization, heavy industrialization under state-owned enterprises, and centralized political control under the Korea Workers' Party. The official state ideology, *juche*, stressed self-reliance (although North Korea did receive aid from the Soviet Union and China), and North Korea's people were isolated from the rest of the world economically and politically. South Korea's path was marked by "guided capitalism" in which the government pushed for the growth of export-oriented industries. Its economic development was aided by billions of dollars in American economic assistance. Such assistance continued even after South Korea's government, originally modeled on American lines, became increasingly authoritarian and fell to a military coup in 1961.

The results of the paths chosen by the two Koreas are two very different societies. A half century after the Korean War, North Korea is a diplomatically isolated, totalitarian regime ruled by Kim Il Sung's son, Kim Jong Il. Its isolation and economic problems intensified when the Cold War ended and the Soviet Union and China cut off their aid to North Korea. Although information about the country is difficult for foreigners to obtain, most observers agree that North Korea is in a state of economic decline or even collapse that has caused widespread poverty and hunger. South Korea, on the other hand, has grown to become the world's eleventh largest economy, with an average annual income of more than $13,000 per person (compared with $900 in North Korea). Its global exports include automobiles and computers. Despite its checkered political history of military coups, authoritarianism, and political protest, it has moved to a more democratic form of government in which presidents and legislatures are elected by the people. Corruption and other economic and political problems remain, but most observers agree that South Koreans have fared better than their northern counterparts.

Despite the immense differences between the two societies and the duration of their separation, many Koreans maintain the dream of eventual reunification. In June 2000, Kim Jong Il and South Korean president Kim Dae Jung met in Pyongyang—the first time leaders of the two nations had met since the Korean War began exactly fifty years earlier. "The Korean people can see a bright future as a dawn of hope for reconciliation, cooperation, and unification is breaking," Kim Dae Jung proclaimed when the historic meeting was concluded. Such hopes faded over the following months as the two countries were unable to follow up the conference with working agreements or further meetings. In addition, some in South Korea accused Kim Dae Jung of compromising too much with the North Korean regime.

The question of Korean reunification has ramifications beyond the Korean peninsula. Both Koreas' neighbors and the United States maintain an active interest in what happens on the Korean peninsula. Since 1953, America has maintained close ties with South Korea, guaranteed its protection, and stationed American troops there (an arrangement that has drawn some protest in South Korea). American relations with North Korea, on the other hand, have ranged from cool to openly hostile, as the United States has accused North Korea of developing nuclear and chemical weapons and of sponsoring terrorism. In 2002 President George W. Bush labeled North Korea as part of an "axis of evil" (along with Iraq and Iran) because of the country's efforts to develop weapons of mass destruction. Divisions exist both within South Korea and in the United States over how much their governments should do to engage the North Korean regime, both to prevent another Korean War and to further the cause of regional peace and possible reunification.

The ongoing division, which has outlasted the Cold War that started it, makes North and South Korea a unique case among nations. *North and South Korea: Opposing Viewpoints* features Korean and foreign scholars and analysts who examine reunification and other prominent Korean issues in the following chapters: Is North Korea a Serious Threat? What Is the State of Democracy and Human Rights in North and South Korea? What Should U.S. Foreign Policy Be Toward North and South Korea? What Is the Future of North and South Korea? The volume provides disparate views about these divergent countries—nations that share much yet are so different.

CHAPTER 1

Is North Korea a Serious Threat?

Chapter Preface

For many years after a 1953 armistice ended the fighting in the Korean War, the scenario most feared by American and South Korean military planners was a reoccurrence of what had started the conflict—a massive invasion of South Korea by North Korea using conventional military forces. To defend and deter against this threat, the United States stationed thousands of American troops in South Korea and pledged to come to that country's aid in the event of attack. More than a million and a half soldiers remain on watch on both sides of the Korean Demilitarized Zone (DMZ) that separates the two countries, ready to fight at a moment's notice. Bill Clinton, on a visit to the DMZ when he was president, declared the region "one of the scariest places in the world."

In recent years, however, concern over North Korea has focused not so much on its conventional military forces and threat of invasion, but on its nuclear weapons program. In 1993 North Korea withdrew from the international Nuclear Non-Proliferation Treaty, provoking an international crisis. After a period of intense negotiations, the United States and North Korea devised an "Agreed Framework" in which North Korea pledged to freeze its nuclear weapons program in exchange for assistance in building civilian nuclear reactors. Despite this agreement, North Korea shook up the world again in 1998 when it test-fired a medium-range ballistic missile over Japan. If North Korea has indeed developed a ballistic missile program, its military reach has been extended to include not only South Korea, but other nations including the United States itself. President George W. Bush and other defense analysts often cite North Korea as a central reason why an American missile defense system is necessary. Not all observers agree, however, about North Korea's nuclear capabilities and intentions. The viewpoints in the following chapter examine some of the debates over the military threat North Korea poses to its neighbor and to the rest of the world.

"North Korea remains the . . . country most likely to involve the United States in a large-scale war."

North Korea Is a Serious Military Threat

U.S. Department of Defense

The following viewpoint contains excerpts from a Department of Defense (DOD) report to Congress on the security situation in Korea. The United States maintains a close security alliance with the Republic of Korea (ROK)—South Korea—to defend against possible invasion or other action by the Democratic People's Republic of Korea (DPRK)—North Korea. The Defense Department holds that the DPRK, despite its poverty, maintains a large military force including ballistic missiles and possible nuclear weapons. It concludes that North Korea remains a major threat not only to South Korea, but to regional stability and United States security.

As you read, consider the following questions:

1. How does the report characterize North Korea's domestic situation?
2. What is North Korea's military goal, according to the authors?
3. What kinds of military hardware does North Korea possess, according to the Defense Department?

Excerpted from "Excerpts of the 2000 Report to Congress, Military Situation on the Korean Peninsula," www.defenselink.mil, September 12, 2000.

N orth Korea remains the major threat to stability and security in Northeast Asia and is the country most likely to involve the United States in a large-scale war. While the [June 2000] historic summit between the North and South leaders [South Korean president Kim Dae Jung and North Korean leader Kim Jong Il] holds the promise of reconciliation and change, no evidence exists of the fundamental precursors for change. There is little or no evidence of economic reform or reform-minded leaders; reduction in military forces; or a lessening of anti-US rhetoric. A decade of steep economic decline has not deterred the North's leaders from allocating precious resources to improving their military forces. The Democratic People's Republic of Korea (DPRK) maintains a dogged adherence to a "military first" policy even against the backdrop of a nation facing severe economic and social challenges.

Leadership

Less than six years after the [1994] death of his father, Kim Jong Il has consolidated power and is firmly in control of North Korea. The leadership continues to focus on its three fundamental themes—regime survival, reunification, and achieving status as a "great and powerful nation." Lacking his father's revolutionary credentials, the North Korean leader relies upon military and security forces to maintain his chokehold on the citizenry. The North Korean leader relies heavily upon military and security forces to maintain his regime. Kim Jong Il sustains regime support by providing resources to key areas at the expense of lower priority sectors of the economy and society. The result is neglect of entire segments of society selected by geography, age, and political reliability. Meanwhile, his inner circle, insulated from the economic and social trauma impacting the lives of ordinary citizens, remains an exclusive group in which relations by blood or marriage, revolutionary ties, and loyalty are the primary prerequisites for power.

Economy

The leadership's most pressing domestic problem is an economy in decline for the tenth consecutive year. The three major components of the North's economic infrastructure—power generation and distribution, communications, and transportation—are failing. Shortages of food, energy, and foreign exchange cripple industry and trade. The underlying cause of the failing economy is the regime's mismanagement of national resources. The regime allows some minor deviations from its centralized policies such as open markets outside government control and limited private agricultural activities. But these are only begrudging adjustments to failure of the central rationing system, and these are not indicative of reform. Until they initiate the major reforms required to create a healthy economic environment, the North will continue to rely on outside help to avert complete economic collapse—and remain an aid-based economy. If economic conditions worsen, we must consider that the North Korean economy could break down completely, precipitating social chaos and threatening the existence of the regime itself. We should anticipate a flood of refugees, humanitarian needs, and the potential for chaos, military coup, or the devastation of civil war. We continue to update our contingency plan to deal with these possibilities. However, the massive economic and infrastructure development aid resulting from the June 2000 summit diminishes the likelihood of this "implosion" scenario.

Military Forces

1. The "Military First" orientation has always been the heart and soul of the North Korean regime. It provides the only conceivable means by which the regime can survive and achieve its ultimate security through reunification. The military continues to grow in both conventional and asymmetrical forces with increasing emphasis on the latter. The military provides deterrence, defense, and a massive offensive threat, as well as leverage in international negotiations. The army is much more than just a military organization; it is North Korea's largest employer, purchaser, and consumer, the central unifying structure in the country, and the source of power for the regime.

2. Pyongyang's military goal is to reunify the peninsula by force. North Korea's fundamental war-fighting strategy mandates achievement of surprise, prosecution of a short

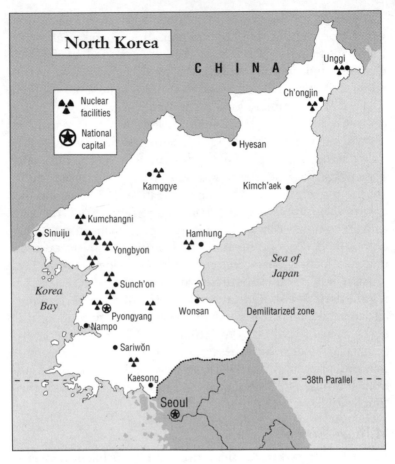

North Korea

- ♠♠ Nuclear facilities
- ✪ National capital

C H I N A

Unggi ♠♠

Ch'ongjin ♠

Hyesan •

•♠ Kamggye

Kimch'aek •

♠♠ Kumchangni

• Sinuiju

Hamhung ♠ •

♠♠ Yongbyon

Sea of Japan

• Sunch'on

Korea Bay

♠♠ ✪ Pyongyang

Wonsan •

Demilitarized zone

• Nampo

• Sariwŏn

♠♠

Kaesong •

--- – – –38th Parallel – – –

Seoul ✪

and violent war, prevention of major United States reinforcement of the peninsula, and negation of the Republic of
Korea's mobilization. The North Korean Armed Forces today are the fifth largest in the world. The ground forces,
numbering one million active duty soldiers, provide the bulk
of the North's offensive war-fighting capability and are the
world's third largest army. They are supported by an air
force of over 1,600 aircraft and a navy of more than 800
ships. Over 6 million reserves augment the active duty personnel. Seventy percent of their active force, to include
700,000 troops, 8,000 artillery systems, and 2,000 tanks, is
garrisoned within 100 miles of the Demilitarized Zone.
Much of this force is protected by underground facilities, including over four thousand underground facilities in the for-

ward area alone. From their current locations these forces can attack with minimal preparations.

3. North Korea fields an artillery force of over 12,000 self-propelled and towed weapon systems. Without moving any artillery pieces, the North could sustain up to 500,000 rounds an hour against [U.S.–South Korean] Combined Forces Command defenses for several hours. The artillery force includes 500 long-range systems deployed over the past decade. The proximity of these long-range systems to the Demilitarized Zone threatens all of Seoul with devastating attacks.

4. Realizing they cannot match Combined Forces Command's technologically advanced war-fighting capabilities, the North's leadership focuses on developing asymmetrical capabilities such as ballistic missiles, special operations forces, and weapons of mass destruction designed to preclude alliance force options and offset our conventional military superiority.

5. The North's asymmetric forces are formidable, heavily funded, and cause for concern. The progress of the North's ballistic missile program indicates it remains a top priority. Their ballistic missile inventory now includes over 500 SCUDs of various types. They continue to produce and deploy medium-range No Dongs capable of striking United States bases in Japan. Pyongyang is developing multi-stage missiles with the goal of fielding systems capable of striking the Continental United States. They tested the 2,000-kilometer range Taepo Dong 1 and continue work on the 5,000 plus kilometer Taepo Dong 2. Pyongyang is one of the world's largest missile proliferators and sells its missiles and technology to anyone with hard currency.

6. In late 1999 North Korea agreed to a moratorium on future missile test firings for the duration of discussions with the US to improve bilateral relations. North Korea publicly reaffirmed that moratorium in June 2000. The US continues to engage North Korea in talks to resolve the threat of North Korean missiles in the region as well as broader concerns with proliferation of North Korean missiles globally.

7. North Korea's Special Operations Forces are the largest in the world. They consist of over 100,000 elite personnel

and are significant force multipliers providing the capability to simultaneously attack both our forward and rear forces.

8. North Korea possesses weapons of mass destruction. A large number of North Korean chemical weapons threaten both our military forces and civilian population centers. We assess North Korea is self-sufficient in the production of chemical components for first generation chemical agents. They have produced munitions stockpiles estimated at up to 5,000 metric tons of several types of chemical agents, including nerve, choking, blister, and blood. We assess that North Korea has the capability to develop, produce, and weaponize biological warfare agents, to include bacterial spores causing anthrax and smallpox and the bacteria causing the plague and cholera. While North Korea denies possession of nuclear weapons and has frozen its nuclear program at Yongbyon, we remain concerned the North could revive a weapons production program. . . .

Deterrence and Defense on the Korean Peninsula

1. The peninsula is viewed as an accurate barometer of the security environment in Northeast Asia, and it remains the most destabilizing factor and largest source of regional tension. The Korean Peninsula is potentially a very volatile arena—dominated by sharp ideological confrontation and backed-up by massive military force. The DPRK is the most critical factor for any positive security developments in Northeast Asia. Unfortunately, the DPRK has chosen to threaten the region with a large build-up of offensive conventional forces and chemical weapons, a quest for nuclear and biological weapons, and the development and sale of ballistic missiles. Until the nuclear issue is fully resolved and the DPRK's conventional military power advantage is reduced, prudent efforts must be continued by the ROK and US to improve overall defense capabilities on the Korean Peninsula.

2. The ROK-US security alliance remains central to the South's overall defense. Additional weaponry can enhance ROK combat power, but it cannot provide the strategic deterrent supplied by a credible US military presence on the Korean Peninsula and timely reinforcement capability. . . .

A Dangerous Theater

The June 2000 summit offers hope to the peninsula that has been absent since 1992. At the time of this writing, it is too early to predict the long-term impact of the summit and North-South dialogues, but it is clear that there has been a significant change on the peninsula. However, continued economic malaise in the DPRK, possible internal security or economic problems and the specter of continued brinkmanship, could contribute to regional instability and result in renewed military aggression by the North. The combined US and ROK forces are a strong and potent deterrent. Until North Korea's conventional military threat is significantly reduced and its quest for nuclear weapons is eliminated, the Korean Peninsula remains a dangerous theater.

> *"The Pentagon . . . needs to portray*
> *North Korea as an unpredictable . . .*
> *enemy . . . as a way to scare Americans*
> *into maintaining . . . its huge military*
> *budget."*

North Korea's Military Threat Has Been Exaggerated

John M. Swomley

John M. Swomley is professor emeritus of social ethics at the St. Paul School of Theology in Missouri and the executive director of the American Committee on Korea. In the following viewpoint, he argues that U.S. government agencies, including the Defense Department and Central Intelligence Agency (CIA), have misled the American people into believing that North Korea is a supremely dangerous military enemy. The extent of North Korea's threat has been exaggerated in order to justify American military spending as well as U.S. control over South Korea, he contends. Swomley blames the United States for diplomatically isolating North Korea and staging war exercises in South Korea to prevent the two countries from improving relations with each other.

As you read, consider the following questions:

1. Why does the Pentagon need to portray North Korea as an enemy, according to Swomley?
2. How has the United States violated the 1953 armistice agreement that halted the Korean War, according to the author?
3. In Swomley's view, why did North Korea reject inspections by the International Atomic Energy Agency?

Bells rang out around the world in March 1999 as an international treaty banning anti-personnel landmines went into effect. Most of the world celebrated the treaty—first signed in Ottawa, Canada, in December 1997—aimed at eliminating tens of millions of the weapons scattered in more than sixty countries and estimated to kill or injure 25,000 people a year, mostly civilians.

In the United States, however, the bells were a call to join the more than 130 signatories and sixty-five nations that had ratified the treaty so far. Although President Bill Clinton has endorsed banning the mines and recently committed funds for disposing of those uncovered by mudslides in Central America in the wake of Hurricane Mitch, he insists that the United States cannot sign the treaty because it still needs the weapons on the Korean peninsula to deter North Korea from invading South Korea. If an alternative to mines can be found, the Pentagon will phase out their use by 2006 and has requested $4.7 million in fiscal 1999 for the search.

But why is North Korea a higher priority for the United States than the international campaign that won the Nobel Peace Prize in 1997? Because the United States is waging a misguided campaign of its own—one that seemingly provides direct and immediate benefits at home but, in the long run, only perpetuates an outdated Cold War mentality that has shackled the peace process.

A Misguided Campaign

Leading this misguided campaign is the Pentagon, which needs to portray North Korea as an unpredictable and dangerous regional enemy in the Pacific as a way to scare Americans into maintaining and increasing its huge military budget. To accomplish this portrayal, the United States government has enforced a more complete embargo on news about and communication with North Korea than for any other country, including Cuba. Even major U.S. newspapers like the *New York Times* are subjected to an intermediary for their information. The CIA and related agencies have become the main sources of data about North Korea, serving "to keep their budgets at hefty Cold War levels," according to Korea expert Professor Bruce Cumings in the January/February

The Pentagon also needs North Korea as an enemy to justify what it calls a "two-war strategy," the other war area being the Middle East. However, this strategy was rejected as unlikely by a national defense panel created by Congress in 1996 to examine future military policy. According to the December 2, 1997, *New York Times*, the panel—made up of four retired generals and admirals and five civilian experts— said the strategy is "a means of justifying the current force structure—especially those searching for the certainties of the Cold War era." The panel recommended diplomacy, not military might, as "the most effective tool" for solving regional conflicts overseas. According to the panel, "The current approach to addressing national security engages the Department of Defense and armed services too often and too quickly."

Without North Korea as an enemy, the Pentagon could not justify continued military and economic control of South Korea. When the new president of South Korea, Kim Dae Jung, came to the United States in June 1998 to win what the *New York Times* reported as

> a more flexible stance [in dealing with North Korea], he made the same argument the Clinton administration has made about China: that the best way [to change North Korea] is not to isolate it and punish it with sanctions but, rather, to build economic and diplomatic ties that draw it out into the international playing field.

Kim's proposal, however, was met with a cool reception not only from the Pentagon but from Congress.

The *Defense Monitor*, published by the Center for Defense Information, which is headed by retired military and naval officers, has long held a view similar to Kim. In January 1994 it concluded:

> The best system is to offer to withdraw U.S. military forces from South Korea in exchange for North Korean abandonment of any nuclear weapons development and agreement to permit unimpeded international inspection to verify the agreement. . . . Establishing diplomatic and economic ties would also encourage a reduction in Cold War hostility.

If it wanted to, the United States could make peace, establish diplomatic relations, and permit hands-on news reporting at any time. Little known is the fact that the United States violated the armistice agreement of July 27, 1953, that ended the Korean War. The armistice provides that

> within three months after the Agreement is signed and effective, a political conference of a higher level of both sides be held by representatives appointed respectively to settle through negotiations the questions of the withdrawal of all foreign forces from Korea, the peaceful settlement of the Korean question.

That agreement, signed by U.S. Army General Mark W. Clark for the United Nations and the United States, is still in force, since the United States has never been willing to end the armistice with a peace treaty. As recently as April 28, 1994, North Korea called on the United States to "replace the Korean Armistice Agreement with a peace treaty" instead of continuing the military confrontation. The armistice also states that the respective military commanders shall

> cease introduction into Korea of reinforcing combat aircraft, armored vehicles, weapons and ammunition; provided however that combat aircraft, armored vehicles, weapons and ammunition which are destroyed, damaged, worn out or used up during the period of the armistice may be replaced on the basis piece for piece of the same effectiveness and the same type.

The United States clearly violated that agreement with the introduction of Patriot missiles into South Korea by presidential order on March 21, 1994, and quite likely led North Korea to develop missiles of its own. North Korea also claims there have been many other violations, including the introduction of nuclear weapons years ago, the introduction of a squadron of Apache helicopters, and the "U.S. naval forces which have clustered" around North Korea.

An imposed state of hostility toward North Korea is in fact evident in a series of military and economic treaties between the United States and South Korea. The Mutual Defense Treaty of October 1, 1953, was designed to provide the United States with an indefinite base for military operations in the north Pacific and to perpetuate a state of war between North Korea and U.S.-occupied South Korea.

Signed immediately after the Korean War, the treaty states that "an armed attack in the Pacific area on either of the Parties in territories now under their respective administrative control" requires that both "act to meet the common danger." Article IV continues: "The Republic of [South] Korea grants and the United States of America accepts, the right to dispose United States land, air and sea forces in and about the territory of the Republic of Korea as determined by mutual agreement." And the countries' fate is sealed in Article VI: "This treaty shall remain in force indefinitely." There must be a one-year notice of any termination.

A False Image

To many, North Korea is the archetypal rogue state, and an old-fashioned communist one at that, motivated to nuclear arm by paranoid hostility to the outside world. Its one-man rule, internal regimentation, and dogmatism would alienate any freedom-loving American. North Korea's brinkmanship, nasty habit of floating concessions on a sea of threats, and harsh diatribes against the United States antagonized even the most impartial observers. So did its past acts of terrorism, like the 1983 bombing in Rangoon that barely missed South Korean President Chun Doo Hwan and killed 17 members of his entourage. The DPRK ceased terrorism and muted its anti-American rhetoric by 1988. Still, the image of a communist rogue state ruled by a latter-day Genghis Khan was difficult to shake. Yes, in many respects, North Korea makes a perfect foe.

The problem with this image is that North Korea has been trying to end its lifelong enmity with the United States since 1988.

Leon V. Sigal, *Harvard International Review*, Summer 2000.

The Mutual Defense Treaty was followed by the Agreed Minutes of November 17, 1954, which specifically obligate South Korea to place its "forces under the operational control of the United Nations Command." This is a euphemism for U.S. control, since there are no other U.N. forces in Korea. In effect, the United States commands not only the 37,000 U.S. troops occupying South Korea but South Korea's own army, navy, air force, and reserves. . . .

On December 13, 1991, North and South Korea signed a nonaggression agreement in which both stated they "shall not interfere in the internal affairs of the other" and "shall refrain from all acts aimed at destroying and overthrowing the other side." They agreed to "discontinue confrontations and competition" and to cooperate in "joint development of resources."

A month later, North Korea signed an agreement permitting the International Atomic Energy Agency (IAEA) to inspect its nuclear facilities. Between May 1992 and January 26, 1993, there were six such inspections.

In spite of this thaw in North-South relations, however, the Pentagon conducted Team Spirit 1993, one of a series of Team Spirit war exercises that have been used over the years to steadily harass North Korea. Team Spirit 1993 lasted more than a month and involved B-1 bombers and warships capable of nuclear strikes as well as more than 200,000 soldiers who practiced an invasion.

As a result of this obvious combined U.S. and South Korean hostility, North Korea announced its decision to withdraw from the Nuclear Non-Proliferation Treaty and rejected IAEA inspections of its military sites. According to the November 20, 1993, *People's Korea*—a Tokyo-based journal edited by Koreans living in Japan and the chief source of official and unofficial news from and about North Korea—North Korea asked to inspect U.S. nuclear weapons and bases in South Korea, saying:

> If we submissively accept an unjust inspection by the IAEA it would be to legitimize the espionage of the United States, a belligerent party vis-a-vis the Democratic People's Republic of Korea, and lead to the beginning of the full exposure of all our military installations.

U.S. War Exercises

Korean sources—including *People's Korea*, which is recognized worldwide as a reliable source—reported that, throughout the negotiations between the United States and North Korea, the Pentagon staged a number of war exercises with South Korea either to intimidate or to practice actual war against North Korea. Even though I have published this information elsewhere, the Pentagon has never denied nor refuted the occurrence of the exercises described:

- August 17, 1993: the United States staged the world's largest super-high-tech simulated nuclear war.

- August 23, 1993: the U.S. aircraft carrier *Independence* staged intensive surprise bombings on strategic offshore areas of North Korea.
- September 23–24, 1993: a formation of U.S. overseas KC-135 tankers refueled some forty fighter-bombers and staged a night air-refueling exercise. Tank groups and artillery units fired hundreds of shells toward areas adjacent to the Demilitarized Zone.
- September 29, 1993: the U.S. Air Force and Navy joined Japan in military exercises directed against North Korea.
- November 15–25, 1993: the United States and South Korea staged a large-scale joint military exercise called Foal Eagle '93, involving 36,000 U.S. troops, 650,000 South Korean troops, and about 1,500 U.S. soldiers from overseas bases.
- December 1–10, 1993: the United States and South Korea staged aerial war exercises involving more than 750 warplanes and refueling tankers with tank groups and artillery units firing shells adjacent to the Demilitarized Zone.
- January 12–14, 1994, and continuing well into 1998: South Korea and the United States, and later the United States alone, staged provocative war exercises preparing to make surprise attacks against the northern half of North Korea using 350 warplanes and armed ground units.

The American press did not report any of these exercises, leaving the impression that North Korea simply would not cooperate with the international community. Instead of reporting this information, some columnists and newspapers even accused the Clinton administration of "being soft on Korea" if it negotiated with, instead of intimidated, the country.

American Imperialism

This naiveté is what results from a successful yet misguided campaign by the U.S. government to shroud its history of military and economic imperialism. Thousands of South Korean students from twenty-one universities and colleges across that country have demonstrated against this imperialism. Korean American political scientist Harold Sunoo acknowledges it in his 1994 book *20th Century Korea:*

> The South Korean economy is completely dominated by for-
> eign capital. All the major Korean firms were built either with
> foreign loans or joint investments with foreign capitalists
> [chiefly U.S. and Japanese]. . . . Wages of the Korean workers
> have remained at the bottom of all Asian countries at a star-
> vation level. . . . Generally speaking, the average Korean
> worker's wage is about one-fifth that of their Japanese coun-
> terparts and one-sixteenth that of American counterparts.

When I visited North Korea in 1994 and again in 1995, I
saw the faces of ordinary people as well as government leaders. North Koreans are not demons to be destroyed but human beings to be respected as any others. And if Americans
were not captive to one-sided reporting, they would seek
change in U.S. policy toward North Koreans. Unfortunately, the U.S. government will never seriously explore
peace as long as it benefits more from war.

"With no defenses, an attack by North Korea could result in tens or even hundreds of thousands of casualties."

A Missile Defense System Is Needed Against North Korea

Paul Wolfowitz

Paul Wolfowitz was appointed deputy secretary of defense by President George W. Bush in 2001. Previously, Wolfowitz served in a variety of academic and diplomatic positions, including assistant secretary of state for East Asian and Pacific affairs under President Ronald Reagan. The following viewpoint is taken from testimony before the Senate Armed Services Committee in July 2001. Wolfowitz argues that the United States needs to develop a system to defend against missile attacks such as those used by Iraq in the 1991 Persian Gulf War. He contends that North Korea is a leading example of a country that has developed missile programs that may be capable of striking the United States with nuclear, chemical, or biological weapons.

As you read, consider the following questions:

1. What scenario does Wolfowitz describe to open his arguments?
2. How much has the number of countries possessing ballistic missiles increased since 1972, according to the author?
3. What does Wolfowitz find disturbing about a North Korean missile test in 1998?

Excerpted from Paul Wolfowitz's testimony before the Senate Armed Services Committee, July 12, 2001.

I magine if you will the following scenario: A rogue state with a vastly inferior military but armed with ballistic missiles and weapons of mass destruction commits an act of aggression against a neighboring country. As President Bush sends forces into the theater to respond, the country's genocidal dictator threatens our allies and deploys forces with ballistic missile attack. Almost without warning, missiles rain down on our troops and pound into densely populated residential neighborhoods of allied capitals. Panic breaks out. Sirens wail as rescue crews in protective gear search the rubble for bodies and rush the injured to hospitals. Reporters mumbling through their gas masks attempt to describe the destruction as pictures of the carnage are instantaneously broadcast around the world.

Mr. Chairman, that scene is not science fiction. It is not a future conflict scenario dreamed up by creative Pentagon planners. It is a description of events that took place 10 years ago [in 1991] during the Persian Gulf War. . . .

I, too, have a vivid recollection of those events. When Iraqi leader Saddam Hussein was launching Scud missiles against Israel, I was sent there with Deputy Secretary of State Lawrence Eagleburger to help persuade Israel not to get drawn further into that war. We saw children walking to school carrying gas masks in gaily decorated boxes; no doubt, to try to distract them from the possibility of facing mass destruction. They were awfully young to be thinking about the unthinkable. With those missiles, Saddam Hussein terrorized a generation of Israeli children and almost succeeded in changing the entire strategic course of the Gulf War.

This year is the 10th anniversary of the first U.S. combat casualties from a ballistic missile attack. In the waning days of Desert Storm, a single Scud missile hit a U.S. military barracks in Dhahran, killing 28 of our soldiers and wounding 99; 13 of them from a single small town in Pennsylvania called Greensburg. For American forces, it was the worst single engagement of the Gulf War. For 13 families in Greensburg, it was the worst day of their lives.

Today, 10 years later, it is appropriate to ask how much better able are we to meet a threat that was already real and serious 10 years ago and has become even more so today.

The answer, sadly, is, not much better. Today our capacity to shoot down a Scud missile is not much improved from 1991 when we deployed . . . , on an emergency basis, the PAC-II missiles to Israel and to Saudi Arabia and other countries.

Terrorism and the Need for Missile Defense

North Korea's nuclear and ballistic missile program underlies an asymmetric deterrence strategy designed to ensure the country's sovereignty by posing a threat to the United States. In the past, this approach would have been considered mainly hypothetical. Today, however, the September 11, 2001 terrorist acts in New York and Washington show that even the United States is vulnerable to outside attack, while such attacks need not come at the hands of a major power. It is also clear that the most serious threat facing the United States in the 21st century is from terrorist groups like al Queda and rogue states like North Korea.

To defend against these threats, the United States will need to maintain "full dimensional protection" and a "full spectrum dominance" military strategy. A key element of the former is an MD [missile defense] system while the latter implies deployment of overwhelming military power to areas of military conflicts. Media commentaries have suggested that the recent terrorist attacks may have undermined support for such a missile defense system. However, it is more likely that September 11 will actually provide impetus for the development of some form of missile defense. Asymmetric strategy inherently involves diverse elements, and certainly a limited nuclear strike with ballistic missiles represents a more disastrous threat than even the recent terrorist attacks. Missile defense is thus a project that the United States is expected to undertake steadily as part of "full dimensional protection."

Lee Jang Wook, *New Asia*, Autumn 2001.

We are still a year or two away from initial deployment of the PAC-III, our answer to the Scud—and, let me add, a very effective answer . . . but we are still many years from full deployment. Today our forces in the Persian Gulf and Korea and the civilian populations they defend have almost no means of protection against North Korean ballistic missiles armed with both chemical and conventional warheads. With no defenses, an attack by North Korea could result in tens or even hundreds of thousands of casualties.

A Real Threat

Mr. Chairman, we underestimated the ballistic missile threat 10 years ago and today, a decade later, we are in danger of underestimating it still. The time has come to lift our heads from the sand and deal with unpleasant but indisputable facts. The short-range missile threat to our friends, our allies and our deployed forces arrived a decade ago. The intermediate-range missile threat is here now, and the long-range threat to American cities is just over the horizon—a matter of years, not decades, away—and our people and our territory are defenseless.

Why? The answer to that last question has four letters: A-B-M-T. ABM [Anti-Ballistic Missile] Treaty [an agreement prohibiting missile defense systems signed by the United States and the Soviet Union in 1972]. For the past decade, our government has not taken seriously the challenge of developing defenses against missiles. We have not adequately funded it, we have not believed in it, and we have given the ABM Treaty priority over it. That is not how this country behaves when we're serious about a problem. It's not how we put a man on the Moon in 10 years. It's not how we developed the Polaris program for intercontinental ballistic missiles in even less time.

The time to get serious is long past. The number of countries pursuing nuclear, chemical and biological weapons is growing. The number of countries pursuing advanced conventional weapons and ballistic missiles is growing. Consider these facts: In 1972, we knew of only five countries that had nuclear weapons. Today [in July 2001] we know of 12 with nuclear weapons programs. In 1972, we knew of a total of nine countries that had ballistic missiles.

Today we know of 28. And in just the last five years more than 1,000 of those missiles of all ranges have been produced. And those are just the cases that we know of. There are dangerous capabilities being developed at this very moment that we know we do not know about and which we may not know about for years, perhaps only after they are deployed.

For example, in 1998 North Korea surprised the world with its launch of a Taepo Dong I missile over Japan with a previously unknown and unanticipated third stage. The intelligence community tells us that this launch demonstrated a North Korean capability to deliver a small payload to the United States. North Korea is now developing the Taepo Dong II missile, which will be able to strike even deeper into U.S. territory and carry an even larger weapons payload. If we do not build defenses against these weapons now hostile powers will soon have or may already have the ability to strike U.S. and allied cities with nuclear, chemical or biological weapons. And they might not even have to use the weapons in their possession to affect our behavior and achieve their ends.

While we have been debating the existence of the threat for nearly a decade, other countries have been busily acquiring, developing and proliferating missile technology. We can afford to debate the threat no longer. We are in a race against time, and we are starting behind. Thanks in no small part to the constraints of the ABM Treaty we have wasted the better part of a decade; we cannot afford to waste another one. [Editor's note: The United States formally withdrew from the ABM Treaty in June 2002.]

"A [negotiated] ban on development . . . of Pyongyang's . . . missiles . . . [would be] a less risky way to counter the threat than unproven missile defenses."

A Missile Defense System Is Not Needed Against North Korea

Leon V. Sigal

Leon V. Sigal argues in the following viewpoint that the threat of ballistic missile attack by North Korea is better addressed with diplomacy than the creation of missile defense systems. North Korea has willingly suspended missile testing and desires a diplomatic solution with the United States, he contends. Negotiating an agreement with North Korea to end its missile threat is a better solution than deploying an untested missile defense system. Sigal is the author of *Disarming Strangers: Nuclear Diplomacy in North Korea*.

As you read, consider the following questions:

1. What does North Korea want in exchange for giving up its missiles, according to Sigal?
2. What has China concluded about the American pursuit of missile defense systems, in the author's view?
3. What initial steps does Sigal believe the United States should take toward North Korea?

From "Korea Summit Provides Opportunities for the United States," by Leon V. Sigal, *San Diego Union-Tribune*, June 15, 2000. Copyright © 2000 by Leon V. Sigal. Reprinted with permission.

In the debate over national missile defense, threat-mongers are hyping the missile menace from so-called "rogue states" to justify spending $60 billion on defenses. Exhibit A for missile-defense proponents has been North Korea.

But the Democratic People's Republic of Korea has refrained from testing a ballistic missile capable of reaching the continental United States, and even worst-case estimates put it a decade away from deploying one. Long before that, Washington could negotiate a ban on development, production and export of Pyongyang's medium- and longer-range missiles—a less risky way to counter the threat than unproven missile defenses.

In a major stride toward such a ban, North Korea agreed last September [1999] to suspend testing while missile talks proceed. It was expected to send a high-level representative to Washington to conduct the talks, assuring equally high-level attention in the U.S. government. In return, the United States announced on Sept. 17 that it would ease its decades-long economic embargo on North Korea.

North Korea has kept its end of the bargain; there has been no untoward activity at its missile test sites since September.

The United States has been slow to reciprocate but is now committed to relaxing sanctions soon. Until it does, however, North Korea's high-level representative will not come to Washington, and lower-level nuclear and missile talks are likely to go nowhere fast.

This week's [June 2000] summit meeting in Pyongyang between South Korean President Kim Dae Jung and North Korean leader Kim Jong Il could improve prospects for a negotiated end to the North's medium- and longer-range missile program.

So could normalization talks between Japan and North Korea, resumed this year after an almost eight-year lapse.

For eight years North Korea has been expressing interest in a missile deal, but it was unwilling to give up its missiles without getting something in return. Most observers took this as a desperate ploy by a regime on the ropes to obtain foreign aid in order to revive its moribund economy. Instead, what North Korea wanted most of all was a political accommodation with the United States, South Korea and Japan to ensure its security.

Other Nations

Tokyo and Seoul recognize that an end to adversarial relations with Pyongyang is the best way to halt proliferation and improve security in Northeast Asia. Moscow and Beijing are also well aware of North Korea's desire for a diplomatic resolution of the missile issue. That is why Russian President Vladimir Putin recently offered to work with the United States to induce North Korea to cease development of longer-range ballistic missiles.

Imminent Threat?

Supporters of building a national missile defense system routinely and matter-of-factly cite the DPRK's [Democratic People's Republic of Korea] imminent ability to launch ICBMs [intercontinental ballistic missiles] laden with nuclear, chemical, or biological warheads onto US soil. . . .

The main evidence for these fears is the DPRK's launch in August 1998 of what was apparently a three-stage rocket. Much was made of the fact that the rocket landed in the Pacific Ocean on the far side of Japan. Press reports, however, contained precious little analysis of how effective the test really was. The third stage failed in its stated design to place a satellite into orbit. Despite this, North Korea has yet to attempt another missile test, due either to political considerations or to lack of resources.

The DPRK's missile capability is also limited in terms of accuracy and payload.

Tim Savage, *Asia Times*, March 4, 2000.

That is also why China has concluded that U.S. missile defenses are aimed at it, not North Korea. "The U.S. is a huge superpower and you're afraid of little North Korea?" Sha Zukang, China's director-general for arms control and disarmament, said recently.

But Washington has yet to come to this realization. U.S. policy-makers must ask themselves why North Korea would move to disarm if the United States remains intent on treating it like a foe.

To negotiate an end to North Korea's missile threat, Washington and Pyongyang need to set political relations on a new course by declaring an end to enmity. As a practical step toward that end, the United States should call off its economic embargo now. In return, North Korea would agree in writing to a formal moratorium on missile testing as a first step toward a comprehensive ban.

Ending adversarial relations with North Korea will put an end to the proliferation danger in Korea. In the late 1980s North Korea's Kim Il Sung decided to reach out to the United States, South Korea and Japan and transform political relations.

Now, for the first time, Washington, Seoul and Tokyo are ready to reciprocate. That will make it possible to put an end to the North Korean missile threat—without deploying untested missile defenses.

Periodical Bibliography

The following articles have been selected to supplement the diverse views presented in this chapter.

Arms Control Today	"North Korea Refuses to Resume Talks with U.S.," September 2001.
Philip C. Clarke	"Preventing Armageddon," *American Legion Magazine*, July 2001.
Nicholas Eberstadt	"The Most Dangerous Country," *National Interest*, Fall 1999.
Selig S. Harrison	"The Missiles of North Korea," *World Policy Journal*, Fall 2000.
Jennifer G. Hickey	"Missiles Alive," *Insight on the News*, March 22, 1999.
Karen Elliott House	"Destitute, Desperate, and Dangerous," *Wall Street Journal*, January 6, 2000.
Marc Lerner	"Korean Roulette," *Reader's Digest*, October 2000.
Bill Mesler	"Why the Pentagon Hates Peace in Korea," *Progressive*, September 2000.
Paik Jin-hyun	"Only North Korea Can Change Its Image as Main Enemy," *Korea Focus*, January/February 2001.
Linda Rothstein	"The Guys Who Cried Wolf," *Bulletin of the Atomic Scientists*, January/February 2000.
Leon V. Sigal	"The Method to the Madness," *Newsweek*, September 13, 1999.
Leon V. Sigal	"Rogue Concepts: Misperceptions of North Korea," *Harvard International Review*, Summer 2000.
Hiromichi Umebayashi	"Northeast Asia Nuclear Weapon Free Zone," *Peace Review*, September 1999.
Michael Wines	"North Korea, with Putin, Vows to Curb Missile Program," *New York Times*, August 5, 2001.

What Is the State of Democracy and Human Rights in North and South Korea?

Chapter Preface

In past decades, outside observers generally found both North Korea and South Korea to be woefully lacking in the areas of democracy and human rights. From 1948 until his death in 1994, Kim Il Sung built up and maintained a dictatorship in North Korea that controlled all aspects of public and private life. Originally based on the Soviet Union's model of Communist dictatorship, it also came to resemble past Korean monarchies, according to some observers, with Kim Il Sung assuming the title of Great Leader. South Korea's government, originally modeled after the United States, was dominated by the military after a group of generals led by Park Chung Hee overthrew the government in 1961. Under Park, South Korea pursued a more market-oriented economic policy than North Korea. However, both Park and his successor, Chun Do Hwan, frequently used their dictatorial powers to limit freedom of speech and the press, suppress government opposition, and maintain their power.

In more recent years, however, the gulf between the human rights records of North and South Korea has widened. In South Korea, rule by military generals has given way to rule under democratically elected presidents and parliamentary members. The presidential elections of former political dissidents Kim Young Sam in 1992 and Kim Dae Jung in 1997 were seen by many as milestones in the transition from military to democratic and civilian rule. South Koreans also enjoy greater freedoms of speech and of the press. North Korea, by contrast, remains "arguably the most tightly controlled country in the world," according to the human rights group Freedom House. "There is little organized dissent as a result of the regime's repression, widespread internal surveillance, and isolationist policies." The North Korean dictatorship survived the 1994 death of its founder, Kim Il Sung; Kim's son, Kim Jong Il, successfully replaced his father as supreme leader of North Korea. While most Communist dictatorships since 1980 have either repudiated communism (as in the case of Russia and the countries of Eastern Europe) or have introduced some measure of economic and political reforms (such as China), North Korea has remained largely closed to the rest of the world and intent on building up its vision of a socialist society. During the 1990s, in addition to reports of human rights abuses, news of widespread hunger and famine suggested that North Korea's government has not only been repressive, but has failed to provide for its people.

Most observers now concur that South Korea has a much better human rights record than its northern neighbor, but differences of opinion remain as to how truly democratic South Korean society is. The following viewpoints provide several perspectives on the state of democracy and human rights in the Korean peninsula.

"The first decade of democratic rule in Korea produced a large number of political . . . reforms."

South Korea Has Achieved Democracy

Larry Diamond and Doh Chull Shin

From 1961 to 1987, South Korea was led by military generals who often ruled by martial law and forcibly quelled political dissent. In 1987, however, student protests compelled military leaders to agree to the popular election of South Korea's president, and a new constitution was approved that made the South Korean government more democratic and protective of political rights. Since then two longtime political dissidents have been elected president—Kim Young Sam in 1992 and Kim Dae Jung in 1997. In the following viewpoint, Larry Diamond and Doh Chull Shin argue that these developments, especially Kim Dae Jung's election, were milestones that marked South Korea's difficult but successful transition from military to democratic rule. South Korea still faces the challenge of consolidating its democratic gains and securing political legitimacy, they concede, but the nation has great promise for achieving a true and lasting democracy.

As you read, consider the following questions:
1. What important events happened in 1997, according to Diamond and Shin?
2. What is the attitude of the South Korean public toward the ideals of democracy, according to the authors?

A mong the dozens of new democracies born during the
so-called third wave of global democratization that began in the mid-1970s, the Republic of Korea is one of the
most politically influential and analytically interesting. With
the eleventh-largest economy in the world, Korea became in
1987 the most powerful democracy in East Asia after Japan.
With a peaceful democratic transition driven by a combina-
tion of a civil society, international pressure, and elite negotiation, followed by almost a decade of relative political stability and continued buoyant economic growth, the country
has often been viewed in the West as a model East Asian
economy and democracy.

During 1997, however, the Korean model was shaken to
its foundations. The popularity of President Kim Young
Sam, the first civilian head of government in three decades
who had entered as a political reformer with wide public
support, collapsed in a series of corruption scandals. Then,
in the last two months of 1997, Korea was struck by its worst
economic crisis in almost half a century. In November, Korea became a symbol of the Asian financial crisis that shook
markets from Hong Kong to Wall Street. With the largest
rescue package ever from the International Monetary Fund
[IMF]—$57 billion—the country was quickly transformed
from an economic powerhouse into a ward of the international financial community.

A Political Breakthrough

Yet economic crisis helped pave the way for a political
breakthrough. On December 18, 1997, Korea became the
first third-wave democracy in East Asia to peacefully transfer power to an opposition party. In that election, the Korean people refused to support the party of a conservative
establishment that had ruled their country for decades in
collusion with military dictators and massive business conglomerates (*chaebols*). Enraged by a financial crisis that subjected their country to unprecedented humiliation and devastating economic misery and pain, Koreans elected as their
president the country's most determined opposition figure,
Kim Dae Jung—a man who had campaigned for the presidency and fallen short three times and who was such an im-

placable foe of the military that he was nearly put to death by the Chun Doo Hwan regime following the May 1980 Kwangju rebellion.

The country's cleanest and most peaceful presidential election in its history took Korea across a visible threshold of democratic maturity. Just five years previously, when Kim Dae Jung contested for the presidency, army generals had openly warned that they would stage a coup rather than allow Kim to become president. This time there was no such talk. Previously, enormous sums of money were used by the ruling party in presidential races to bribe voters. This time, the ruling party distanced itself from such dirty money politics.

Kim Dae Jung's victory ranks in political significance with the election of such other courageous democratic dissidents as South Africa's Nelson Mandela and Poland's Lech Walesa. Undoubtedly Kim's electoral victory represents a major turning point in Korea's journey toward a fully consolidated democracy. It also marks the transition to a new era of democracy in East Asia. Asian democracy has often been equated largely with rule by a dominant, single party that brooked limited opposition. Even if one does not doubt the willingness of a long-dominant party to surrender power if it loses an election, the actual moment represents a qualitative change in the character and vibrancy of democracy. In Korea, however, this remarkable change has coincided with (and was probably made possible by) a profound economic crisis. That crisis has revealed the dark side of the Korean model of democracy and prompted serious debates over whether political democracy can coexist with crony capitalism for any extended period of time.

Important Reforms

On his election, Kim Dae Jung quickly moved to support financial reform bills mandated by the IMF loan deal. He demanded the fundamental restructuring of governmental agencies and major conglomerates, which control over three-quarters of Korea's gross domestic product. At the same time, he began to tame the most powerful labor unions in Asia, which had pushed wages up fivefold in the previous decade, seriously undermining the "miracle" of Korea's export-led growth. In short, Kim Dae Jung's endeavors to restructure crony capitalism and the old way of running politics signaled true change and began to dispel the view that democratically elected governments in Korea could not implement fundamental economic reforms.

In fact, the first decade of democratic rule in Korea produced a large number of political and economic reforms reshaping the institutions and procedures of military-authoritarian rule into those of representative democracy. Laws were passed to promote free and fair electoral competition at all government levels. Three free and competitive presidential elections were conducted, the third of which produced a historic rotation of power. Three rounds of parliamentary elections also enabled the people to choose their representatives to the National Assembly. In local communities, popularly elected governors and legislators have taken the place of appointees of the central government.

Korea thus has fully restored civilian rule by extricating the military from power. Also Korea has fully established the other minimal architecture of procedural democracy—a political regime practicing free and fair elections, universal adult suffrage, multiparty competition, civil liberties, and a free press. It is also an increasingly liberal democracy, one of only six countries in Asia that is rated "free" by Freedom House.

The Notion of Democratic Consolidation

In Korea today, there is general agreement that electoral politics has become the only possible game in town. The successful establishment of electoral democracy, however, cannot be equated with the consolidation of Korean democracy. To become consolidated, democracy must achieve deep, broad, and lasting legitimacy at three levels: political elites, politically significant parties and organizations, and the mass public. At each level, actors must manifest both a normative commitment to democracy as the best form of government (or at least better than any imaginable alternative) and a behavioral commitment to comply with the specific rules and procedures of the constitutional system. Often this requires (or may be facilitated by) some redistribution of political and socioeconomic resources, but at bottom democratic consolidation involves political leadership and institution building.

In new democracies, like the one in Korea, where in the past the military ruled for decades, holding competitive elections and reestablishing representative institutions alone cannot bring about significant changes in the redistribution of political power and other valued resources. Nor can the formal (electoral) institutions of democracy be expected to ensure adequate protection for human rights or the political incorporation of previously marginalized groups.

Lurie's Newscartoon. © 2000 by Cartoonews International Syndicate, N.Y.C., USA. Reprinted with permission.

This is why the constitutional order is profoundly important to the quality and stability of democracy and thus why consolidation requires both appropriate institutional designs and an independent judiciary capable of enforcing the constitution and the rule of law. All these dynamics in turn heavily affect how the mass public views democracy and whether it will become deeply and intrinsically committed to its legitimacy. Democratic consolidation will advance to the extent that the political institutions of democracy are deepened and improved to become more open, responsive, accountable, and respectful of the law and to the extent that democracy is seen by the mass public to be delivering the political goods it promises: freedom, justice, transparency, participation, and a predictable, stable, constitutional order.

The transition from authoritarian military rule, holding free and fair elections, and installing a new electoral democracy encompass well-defined, single tasks. In sharp contrast, the consolidation phase is confronted with a multitude of diverse and pressing institutional and policy challenges: corruption, the crimes of the authoritarian past, lawlessness, feeble judicial systems, ineffectual bureaucratic institutions, a fragmented political party system, deep-seated regional or ethnic divisions, growing social inequality, and now a profound economic crisis. . . .

Toward Consolidation?

Korea has been one of the more vigorous members in the family of third-wave democracies. Several waves of institutional and legal reforms have been carried out in order to establish the necessary institutions and procedures of representative democracy and to rectify the wrongs of the authoritarian past. Although not all these reforms have been equally successful and much remains to be done, Korea has firmly institutionalized the two most important principles of procedural democracy: free and fair electoral competition and civilian supremacy over the military. For Korea and for East Asia, the presidential election victory in 1997 of a lifelong democratic dissident and opposition leader who was almost put to death by the military and his assumption of office without incident represent a particular milestone on the path to democratic maturity.

Yet for all the reforms it has pursued and adopted during its first decade of democracy, Korea remains far from a consolidated, liberal democracy. The mass public is committed to the ideals of democracy but shows some growing ambivalence about whether democracy is the best system for Korea in this troubled time. Elites remain more divided than united, even over the basic structure of democratic governance. . . .

At the level of elite behavior, governmental and nongovernmental forces alike often appear unwilling to abide by all the rules (written and unwritten) of the democratic game, including those of accountability and transparency. As revealed in a series of major scandals involving the two democratically elected former presidents, Roh Tae Woo and Kim Young Sam, the formal norms of accountability and constitutionalism remain overpowered by the informal norms of clientelism, cronyism, and personalism. Both elected officials and their representative institutions are yet to be dissociated from the various legacies of the authoritarian past.

Korea remains far from a fully liberal state even after a decade of democratic rule, although it is one of the most pluralistic nations in Asia. Citizens in the South, for example, are still not free to visit, without governmental permission, North Korea's home page on the Internet, not to mention owning its books and magazines. Even those who try to listen to North Korean radio broadcasts continue to be imprisoned under the National Security Law that was promulgated in 1948. According to Minkahyup, a human rights group in Korea, there were 478 political prisoners in Korean jails when Kim Dae Jung took office. This number is not known to have been reduced to any significant degree. Under the democratic Sixth Republic, as in the authoritarian past, tolerance of communism remains "an unaffordable luxury" among ordinary citizens, despite their president's "sunshine" policy toward North Korea.

What can and should be done to deepen, liberalize, and consolidate democracy in Korea? Along with responding to the economic crisis, this is the most serious challenge the Kim Dae Jung government now faces. . . .

The consolidation of democracy in Korea will no doubt be advanced by generational change as well. In all likelihood, Kim Dae Jung will be the last president of the political generation that led the struggles for and against Korea's developmental authoritarian state. With the emergence of a new generation of political party leaders, there is the chance that the agenda for political and economic reform will gather momentum. In this respect, ironically, Kim Dae Jung—once derided as a dangerous leftist—may now be laying the foundation for deeper and more sustainable reform by opening Korea more fully to the economic and social forces of globalization. His ambitious agenda for economic, political, and social reform coincides with and is reinforced by a renewed flourishing of Korean civil society. If, through a process of dialogue and negotiation with business and labor, Kim Dae Jung can succeed in restructuring and opening up the economy, while buffering the pain for the roughly two million Koreans who will have to cope with unemployment during this wrenching transition, he will not only rekindle economic growth. He will alter the political and economic culture of Korea in ways that will benefit the consolidation of its maturing but still awkward democracy.

> *"It is evident that the quest for democratization . . . [remains a] real but somewhat distant . . . [goal] for the Republic of Korea."*

South Korea Has Not Yet Achieved Democracy

John Kie-chiang Oh

John Kie-chiang Oh is a professor of politics at Catholic University of America and the author of *Korean Politics: The Quest for Democratization and Economic Development*, from which the following viewpoint is excerpted. He argues that the Republic of (South) Korea has, after decades of autocratic and military rule, attained a level of "procedural" democracy in that its political leaders are chosen by popular election. However, despite the significant economic and political changes over the past half century, he asserts that South Korea has yet to create a stable two-party system or a secure foundation for a genuine democratic society. Economic turmoil, he argues, might wipe away past gains toward democratization.

As you read, consider the following questions:

1. What two cultural traditions influence Korean political culture, according to Oh?
2. How have Korean citizens reacted to arrogant and dictatorial government leaders, according to the author?
3. How has South Korea been transformed since 1948, according to Oh?

The end of the Second World War witnessed a tidal wave of Western democracy on many shores including those of Japan, where American occupation authorities hurriedly wrote a "model" democratic constitution in the name of the Japanese people. A small group of Koreans, whose backgrounds indicated little familiarity with a democratic system of government, likewise drafted a constitution that declared "Korea shall be a democratic republic," under a not-so-subtle nudge by the American military government in South Korea. Thus "democracy" became the founding ideology for the Republic of Korea, when it was inaugurated as the American military occupation there ended in 1948. Meanwhile, in North Korea, then under Soviet occupation, Communism was dictated as the ruling ideology. Thus began the trial of democracy in the South, which was desperately poor and constantly concerned about her security in her precarious geopolitical position. The Korean War followed two years later, making South Korea a garrison state.

Korea's Undemocratic Past

Prior to the establishment of the republic, Korean politics had hardly been democratic. A long dynastic past was succeeded by a militarist occupation by Japan, which in turn was replaced by the American military occupation. Traditional political culture in Korea was essentially feudal, elitist, and authoritarian, albeit not without some populist, protodemocratic elements such as the *Tonghak* [Eastern Learning] ideals. [The *Tonghak* Movement was a nineteenth-century political and religious movement of Korean farmers.]These spread rapidly and widely among numerous peasants toward the end of the nineteenth century and left an indelible imprint on the political consciousnesses of numerous Koreans. The principal legacies of the traditional political culture, therefore, were largely authoritarian and elitist on the one hand, and populist and protodemocratic on the other. At the risk of overgeneralizing, the former, which lasted for a much longer period than the latter, may be called the Confucian tradition and the latter the *Tonghak* tradition. Tension and frequent conflict between the two traditions continued to unfold throughout the life of the Republic of Korea, sometimes perhaps giving the impression to outsiders that a Korean is at once an authoritarian and a democrat. Examples of just that abound, including Syngman Rhee who apparently became a "Confucian" autocrat surrounded by *yangban* [aristocratic] officials as he was elected the first president of South Korea, and President Kim Dae-jung who has repeatedly and explicitly identified himself with the *Tonghak* tradition. One might add that a Korean citizen is at once a Confucian and a populist, among other things.

From another perspective, a fundamental problem has been the huge gap between the elaborate "republican" superstructure, which was hurriedly erected in 1948, and the largely authoritarian and underdeveloped substructure of Korean politics. On the morrow of the establishment of the republic, this abysmal gap was to occasion numerous tragicomic incongruities. For decades it caused painful dislocations and necessitated drastic adjustments in South Korean politics and government. This gap, however, has narrowed considerably in recent decades. In the past fifty years [since 1998] the legal-institutional features have been modified, partly through constitutional amendments and changes in institutional structures and procedures. At the same time, the increasingly better-educated people have become gradually familiar with many democratic processes while learning to abhor dictatorial practices.

It is striking that democracy has remained for the past half a century a persistent and strong aspiration—initially among intellectuals and elites but gradually spreading to the expanding middle class and beyond. Historically Koreans have manifested a tendency to intensify what they acquire and choose to believe in. For instance, many Korean Confucianists were more Confucian than Confucius, and many Korean Christians today may be more Christian than Christ. Likewise, numerous Korean "democrats" in recent decades have fought for democracy, arguably with more determination than did Thomas Jefferson. The quest for democratization continues in South Korea, and that drive has resulted in the recent peaceful transfer of power to an opposition presidential candidate who opposed authoritarianism for nearly fifty years.

Economically, a vast majority of Koreans led a life of genteel poverty for generations. Japanese colonial domination left the Korean economy debilitated and disjointed after the Pacific War. The American occupation barely kept South Korea alive, and two years after the establishment of the Rhee government, which was largely indifferent to economic matters while preoccupied with nation and state building, came three years of the devastating Korean War.

South Korean Politics

South Korean politics is very democratic in that Western-style elections are conducted peacefully, and freedom of the press, of political assembly and expression are guaranteed. However, South Korean politics is very undemocratic in several ways: an imperial presidency still prevails, the National Assembly is very much under the president's tight control, and the press censors itself. Further, the freedom of political assembly and expression is often violent.

Yearn Hong Choi, *Los Angeles Times*, February 6, 2000.

The war and persistent security obsessions left South Korea with the fourth largest standing army in the world, and so it was not surprising that disgruntled or reform-minded elements would plot the overthrow of the civilian regimes that became harshly autocratic in the case of the Rhee regime and dysfunctional in the case of the [1960–1961] Chang Myŏn government. The 1960 "righteous student uprising" that toppled the Rhee administration was spontaneous, somewhat like the *Tonghak* peasants' rebellions, against an autocratic and oppressive regime that had lost its legitimacy in the eyes of the people. It set a precedent of successfully overthrowing an unjust or ineffectual regime.

Military Coup

The military coup d'etat of 1961 led by Park Chung Hee was the first military putsch with the cynically twisted justification of restoring "democracy," assuring national security, and reviving the economy. What turned out to be a thirty-year military-dominated authoritarian rule thus began, justifying its legitimacy and prolongation of the military rule in the name of rapid but colossally unbalanced economic growth. It is an undeniable fact, nevertheless, that the strong developmental state led by Park triggered spectacular economic growth, giving rise in time to a large middle class and, with it, an energized civil society. Thus the unprecedented economic growth that was generally sustained under another former general contained the seeds of the destruction of military dictatorship and of the structural distortions and problems rooted in government-business collusion.

Ordinary citizens seemed to accept, almost fatalistically, a great degree of government control and even oppression in the name of economic growth and national security. However, when the various governments became overly arrogant and dictatorial, intellectuals, many religious leaders, opposition leaders and their parties, educated middle-class citizens in numerous urban centers, students largely from middle-class backgrounds, workers, and other members of the increasingly active civil society repeatedly and valiantly struggled to protect and reassert their democratic rights. Until very recently they were practicing "protective democracy." While they were struggling against dictatorships their slogan was "Fight for Democracy!" and soon they became self-professed believers in democracy, although the concept itself was seldom carefully analyzed beyond the textbook level by these "democracy fighters." Political parties remained ephemeral. Individual political leaders, including Kim Young Sam and Kim Dae-jung among others, courageously and single-mindedly led these struggles for democracy for decades. Initially democracy had been a "gift" of the American military occupation in South Korea. However, millions of Koreans demonstrated all over South Korea intermittently for decades to defend the country against dictators, both civilian and military. The student uprising of 1960, the Kwangju uprising of 1980, and the mammoth people's march of 1987 are but the most spectacular examples. Hundreds of democracy fighters even gave their lives for the cause. Numerous others were wounded or suffered in some other ways. For instance, Kim Young Sam fasted for about three weeks, and Kim Dae-jung, who was almost killed by military dictators three times, was imprisoned for six years and exiled twice. What the South Koreans fought for and retained is genuinely their own.

The United States, the "prime mover" of Korean democracy and the principal defender along with South Koreans of the republic during the war, usually sided with those Koreans who struggled to retain and nurture democracy. However, during the cold war era the primary priority of the United States was security in and around Korea. Much anti-Americanism there was due to the perception by young Koreans that the United States was supporting dictatorial regimes in Korea, where tens of thousands of American soldiers are stationed even today to contribute to the country's security.

The People Act

In a relatively secure and stable Korea, civil groups and ordinary voters participated in politics with increasing sophistication. For instance, when three political leaders merged their parties in 1990 in a Machiavellian marriage of convenience and created a superruling party in the National Assembly under President Roh [Tae Woo] , the people in effect nullified the merger by defeating the ruling party in the 1992 National Assembly elections. The election of a "civilian and democratic" president in 1992 finally marked the end of the military domination of politics. However, when that government became self-righteous and arrogant, the outcome of the 1995 local government elections, in which the government party was decisively defeated, once again proved voter sophistication and adumbrated a transfer of power to an opposition camp. In time the Korean nation has made democracy—at least procedural democracy—its own by regularly electing freely and fairly its representatives and presidents. The election of an opposition candidate as president in 1997 clearly marked an historic turning point in the evolution of Korean politics.

In this evolution, however, political parties remain the weakest link. Fifty years after the establishment of the republic political parties are still essentially loose coalitions of politically active individuals organized around strongwilled and identifiable political leaders or bosses. They still do not articulate, with any degree of consistency, political principles or action plans. Parties are largely based on patron-client relations and they form, merge, split, and disappear with the movements and political fortunes of these patrons. Though the number of these groupings has definitely shrunk in recent decades, and some intraparty procedures, such as candidate nomination processes, are gradually regularized, South Korea still does not have anything approaching a stable two-party system. Until political parties become stable and predictable, the South Korean political arena will probably remain volatile.

In sum, despite fluctuations and setbacks, the political and economic transformations of South Korea have been extraordinary. The transfiguration of the past fifty years has been far more revolutionary than the changes that took place in Korea for thousands of years before that. Democracy is showing sufficient vital signs today to indicate that it is not only surviving but taking root in the southern part of the divided Korean peninsula and has met the test of attaining procedural democracy by "kicking the rascals out" of office and installing a genuine opposition group. Democracy has passed the stage of being merely a founding and legitimizing ideology and an aspiration. Indeed, the turbulent, zigzagging, and sometimes bloody quest for democratization has recently experienced a constrained transition and movement toward consolidation.

Korea's Economy

The Korean economy, largely agricultural until the mid-1960s, has become essentially a manufacturing and a capitalist economy and experienced unprecedented and generally sustained growth under the direction of a developmental state until the late 1980s. However, the economy has recently suffered from long-accumulated structural problems and systemic corruption, and is facing the urgent needs of drastic structural readjustments and the elimination of corruption largely attributable to government business collusion. For too long the state remained authoritarian, and the top leadership positions of most *chaebŏl* [South Korea's largest corporations] were occupied by the original, and sometime legendary, founders of these conglomerates, Confucian patriarchs or veritable "monarchs" of huge manufacturing and business empires. Business tycoons colluded with political leaders and created what might be called a *"chaebŏl republic,"* whose tangled webs of power and money could not be broken until a powerful external force, the IMF [International Monetary Fund], urgently intervened days before South Korea faced sovereign insolvency. Business practices and state-business collusion precluded accountability and transparency, the phenomenon that created the illusion of invincibility in the Korean economy among the top government bureaucracy, *chaebŏl* executives, and investors, both foreign and domestic—until shrewd international speculators began withdrawing their investments from South Korea. The state-economy interplay, which once had created a thriving "Korea, Inc.," rapidly degenerated as both sides became authoritarian, unaccountable, greedy, and corrupt.

The state-business interplay was continuous, significant, and often interactive—both positively and negatively. When economic activities lacked sociopolitical recognition and rewards during the Rhee era, for instance, the economy remained inactive and anemic. It took a determined military-led regime to trigger rapid economic growth, and another authoritarian-bureaucratic regime to sustain it. For nearly two decades, beginning in the mid-1960s, the interaction was generally positive and productive, strictly in economic terms. However, from the perspective of democratization, political development and economic growth were often inversely correlated. In other words, political development in terms of democratization and the advancement of human rights suffered severely under the strong developmental regimes, with the dreaded intervention of the ubiquitous Korean Central Intelligence Agency, subsequently called the Agency for National Security Planning—and now in the Kim Dae-jung administration, the Agency for Intelligence Service. Most recently, political democratization has reached a high point while the economy is experiencing a catastrophe, again in an inverse pattern, for the present. Just as the evolution of democracy elected a president from the opposition camp, the economy was shaken to its foundations due to long-accumulated problems. While the new deadlock-prone government, business conglomerates, and labor are responding sluggishly to the economic cataclysm, it was remarkable symbolically that the "free" citizens, largely of the middle class, voluntarily responded under the aegis of civil society groups to the economic crisis, as in the gold collection campaign and various voluntary belt-tightening measures.

However, it appears that the worst may be yet to come. When large-scale restructuring and the survival of only the fittest enterprises occur, they are bound to produce wave after wave of unemployed citizens in a society with sparse safety nets. The quest for economic development has been frustrated in catastrophic proportions, and the crisis might last for years. The economic position of the middle class, an element of stability and often a liberalizing force during the last decade, may be seriously eroded. The unemployed and angry might suffer in relative silence for a while, as they have in the past under political suppression; however, they also have a history of taking to the streets, sometimes violently. Social and political consequences of such disturbances might be far reaching, particularly if the newly installed government were to come under a siege mentality and overreact against, for instance, labor strikes. Much of the political gains in terms of democratization might be quickly wiped out, and the limits of democracy in Korea might yet be exposed in an unfortunate interplay of the economy and politics. Such are the challenges that the Kim Dae-jung government, essentially a coalition regime with an unstable legislature, faces at this [1999] writing.

A Distant Goal

Political and economic turning points have been reached almost simultaneously. It will take all the genius and resources of the Korean leaders and the people alike to overcome the worst national crisis since the Korean War. It is evident that the quest for democratization, beyond the stage of procedural democracy, and the quest for sustainable and equitable economic development, remain real but somewhat distant and idealized goals for the Republic of Korea.

"People's Korea not only has an impressive record of past achievement, but still has much to offer its people that many other societies endowed with greater material wealth do not."

North Korea's Government Has Served Its People Well

Hugh Stephens

Hugh Stephens is a political and anti-imperialist activist who has written extensively on Libya and Iraq as well as North Korea. He is secretary of the Institute for Independence Studies, based in London, England. The following viewpoint is excerpted from an article he wrote after visiting the Democratic People's Republic of (North) Korea in 1998 on its fiftieth anniversary. Stephens writes that North Korea's people remain enthusiastic supporters of the government and have been well served by the "Juche idea" of independent socialism. He argues that the Juche idea, developed by longtime North Korean leader Kim Il Sung and carried on by his son, Kim Jong Il, is the key to understanding North Korea's success in maintaining its socialist revolution even as the Soviet Union and countries in Eastern Europe have abandoned it.

As you read, consider the following questions:
1. What have been some of the accomplishments of North Korea's government, according to Stephens?
2. What are some of the main philosophical concepts of the "Juche idea," according to the author?
3. According to Stephens, what lessons does North Korea impart to the rest of the world?

S eptember 9, 1998 was the fiftieth anniversary of the foundation of the Democratic People's Republic of Korea. On that day, there took place in the Republic's capital city of Pyongyang what must surely be ranked among the most remarkable and high-spirited affirmations of revolutionary optimism in our time.

Throughout the morning, serried ranks of incomparably well-drilled military formations paraded through the town, while in the afternoon hundreds of thousands of schoolchildren performed impeccably-rehearsed mass athletic displays, followed at night by a massive torchlight procession by the citizens of Pyongyang. Altogether, perhaps two million people participated in these events, and this was besides parades, demonstrations and displays in the Republic's other towns. At the morning's military parade all eyes were turned on Kim Jong Il, who had that week been re-elected as Chairman of the Military Defence Commission of the Supreme People's Assembly, the position from which he will be conducting his leading role in affairs of state. Another note of exhilaration was added to this occasion by the fact that some days earlier People's Korea had undertaken its first satellite launch, a truly remarkable achievement for a small developing country under siege.

To attend these celebrations was an unforgettable experience that could not fail to awaken all kinds of reflections not only on People's Korea itself but on the state of the world as a whole. As the storms of financial and economic crisis swept across the capitalist-dominated world, here was a people offering a vision of another way, a socio-political system proudly displaying its confidence in the future, rallied around its leadership in an astounding display of unity, and proudly upholding its own chosen path of socialism and anti-imperialism as an alternative to the gloomy outlook and dog-eat-dog morality offered by capitalism.

Confidence Amidst Hardship

This confidence and determination was all the more remarkable considering the intensity of the hardships and difficulties currently being faced by the very people who were engaged in these celebrations. Catastrophic natural disasters, from droughts to unprecedented floods and devastation, have in recent years afflicted many countries of Asia, and People's Korea has been among the worst affected. Barely forty-eight hours before the anniversary celebrations, the sky above Pyongyang had darkened, bringing darkness in daytime in such a threatening and eerie manner that it was hard to believe one was on planet Earth. Soon the sky opened, and three hours of torrential rainfall turned streets into rivers, and cars, up to their axles and above in water, seemed in danger of floating away. The following day, on a visit to rural areas, we saw crops flattened, mud-slides and subsidence making roads impassable, telegraph poles down, and men, women and children all out in force working with a will to make emergency repairs to ruptured dikes and blocked roadways. A report by the Korean Central News Agency stated that scores of people had lost their lives as a result of this storm, while CNN, who had a team on hand to cover the celebrations, brought harrowing images of bereaved families and devastated villages to the world's television screens.

These natural disasters have come at a time when the socialist trade system of which the trade of People's Korea formed a part for over forty years has come to an end, unexpectedly facing it with the difficult task of establishing a new pattern and new methods of international commerce at the most difficult of moments, and all this at a time when the US blockade, the longest blockade of any country in the whole of history, is being intensified and is wreaking its vindictive worst.

The people celebrating on the streets of Pyongyang and the other towns of People's Korea were therefore inevitably far from being oblivious to the trials they must endure on their chosen path, suffering as they are their period of most severe privation since the years of war and its aftermath in the 1950s.

How can it be that, despite enduring such material hardship, a people can give such massive endorsement to their socialist system and its leadership at a time when nearly ten years have passed since, like ninepins, the socialist states of Eastern Europe fell as a result of rejection by their people? This resilience of Korea's socialist system is particularly remarkable given the passing away in July 1994 of Kim Il Sung, the historic leader from whom Korean socialism derived so much of its prestige and standing both at home and abroad.

A North Korean View on Human Rights

The concept of human rights in North Korea . . . [is] different from the common concept of human rights. The North Korean concept of human rights is inseparably linked with the principle of "our way of socialism," Juche-ism, as well as the totalitarian view of value and is transformed by them. The party's dictionary strongly and blatantly endorses the relativity of human rights to the socialist system by explaining human rights as:

> Rights which men are entitled to as human beings become their independent rights and human rights as social beings are expressed within their political, economic and cultural lives. Human rights are only completely guaranteed when various forms of exploitation and suppression are cleared away, and in a social system where the people are the host.

Sung-Chul Choi, ed., *Understanding Human Rights in North Korea*, 1997.

Despite the constant predictions of its imminent collapse that have been made throughout the past decade, People's Korea not only has an impressive record of past achievement, but still has much to offer its people that many other societies endowed with greater material wealth do not. The benefits of living in a politically-united society are in themselves considerable. This is by no means a matter of moral satisfaction alone, as the numerous countries which have been or are threatened or engulfed by civil conflict and war during these past decades could testify. The economy, for many years the basis of a level of people's welfare which was deeply impressive to visitors from other developing countries, has continued to respond creatively to the people's needs. Even at its present time of greatest trial, it has sustained basic human requirements including emergency relief, and has attracted favourable comments from many international aid personnel who have been working there. In the field of culture, the educational system of People's Korea is quite simply unparalleled by any other country of comparable material resources: the standard of infant care and junior education has on many occasions attracted the praise of visitors from many lands, while the recent satellite launch is only one of many achievements which demonstrate the accumulated skill of its scientists and technicians. In the field of national defence, People's Korea has for forty-five years faced down the US and its allies, sustaining a level of military preparedness which has protected its citizens from a renewal of the hostilities which ended in 1953.

These continuing achievements in the fields of politics, economics, culture and national defence provide the basis on which the claim can be sustained that Korea's unique people-centred socialism provides an alternative path to submission to domination by capitalism and imperialism, a path which provides its people with a decent life in which, despite the present material privations, they share weal and woe with their fellows, hold their heads high and work with confidence and determination for a better future.

Fifty Years of Confronting Imperialism

In order to explore more deeply the reasons for the resilience of the Korean socialist system, it is necessary to trace the history of Korean socialism back to its origins and appreciate its particular significance in the global confrontation of capitalism and socialism. Above all, it is necessary to gain an understanding of the historic role of Kim Il Sung and his original ideology, the Juche idea, and of the role of Kim Jong Il in systematising this ideology in such a way as to successfully take the cause forward into the new generation.

First of all, People's Korea stands very firmly in the socialist tradition. It was established in the period of worldwide socialist advance following the defeat of the Axis powers at the end of the second world war, being one of a number of Asian socialist states established at that time. It is these socialist states in Asia which, along with socialist Cuba, have proved the most steadfast in continuing along the socialist road, and upon which the future of world socialism now largely depends. People's Korea has played a distinguished role in world socialist history, defending the Eastern frontier of the socialist world for half a century, a role which it has performed with great distinction and at the cost of great self-sacrifice. The distinctive nature of Korean social-

ism which consciously cultivates its own national characteristics should not be allowed to obscure the fact that People's
Korea continues unerringly on the path of socialist interna-
tionalism and has always identified its cause with that of the
other socialist countries and with the cause of world socialist revolution as a whole.

This standpoint, besides earning People's Korea the gratitude and solidarity of the world's socialists and all progres-
sive people, has by the same token earned it the hatred and
vindictiveness of US imperialism and its allies, particularly
since their failure to subdue it in the war of 1950 to 1953.
The prolonged blockade which has left People's Korea in
such a bad position to withstand the setbacks to world socialism and the national disasters of recent years, has been
repeatedly punctuated with serious and dangerous crises
provoked by the US, and massive and threatening US and
allied military exercises have kept the clouds of war hovering
over the Korean peninsula to this day. Even just to admit the
existence of People's Korea has evidently been a problem not
only for the US imperialists but also for their junior partners
in Britain; as late as the 1980s, Britain's Foreign Office declared that "we do not recognise North Korea as a country
nor the authorities operating there as a government."

With an enemy which in such ways openly indicated that
it was not prepared to regard People's Korea as anything
more than a blank space on the map, its people came to at-
tach an enormous significance to the historic leading role of
Kim Il Sung, who symbolised their defiance of imperialist
threats, their refusal to renounce their national identity, and
their collective will to chart their own path towards socialism and national reunification. The standing and prestige of
Kim Il Sung as the focus of the Korean people's revolutionary loyalty and of the national identity which imperialism
sought to obliterate reached a degree that is unfamiliar, indeed totally unknown, almost anywhere else. Possessed of a
uniquely indomitable will, a total identification with the Korean people's cause, and a mind of truly great originality,
Kim Il Sung perfectly fulfilled his role. His sixty-and-more
years of political activity at the head of the Korean revolution, during which time he led his people to victory over two

imperialist powers, established a uniquely close bond between leader and people.

During his long years at the helm of the revolution, Kim
Il Sung developed the Juche idea, a distinctive and original
ideology embracing the whole range of theory and practice
of revolution and construction. . . .

The Juche Idea

The Juche idea derives its origin from two simple propositions: first, that a revolution can only be advanced by going
among the people, arousing and educating them, and enlist-
ing their strength; secondly, that the revolution in each
country must be carried out in an independent and creative
way by its own people and not in response to demands or approval from outside. . . .

These simple propositions, advanced by Kim Il Sung
while still in his teens, were the starting-points of the Juche
idea, which during the next sixty-and-more years he applied
to the whole range of theory and practice of revolution and
socialist construction, resulting in the development of theo-
retical and practical applications throughout the spheres of
politics, economics, culture and national defence. . . .

It is not easy to gain an appreciation of the elaborate conceptual framework and wide-ranging practical application of
the Juche idea, but any serious assessment of People's Korea
and its socialist system requires at least some familiarity with
the terms and concepts used.

The Juche idea puts forward a new definition of people,
that they are social beings with the properties of independence, creativity and consciousness. On the basis of this
definition, it raises a new fundamental question for philosophy, namely the relation of people to the surrounding
world, and puts forward the answer that people dominate
and transform it, or that 'people are masters of everything
and decide everything'. . . .

The definition of people advanced by the Juche idea is
based on the fact that people are the only social beings, in
that a person's essential nature is formed in social relations
with other people. Hence, people's properties are not in-
born; they are created through social life and develop his-

torically. The independence property is the aspiration of people to live and develop independently as masters of the world and their own destiny, and to submit neither to natural nor social constraints. The property of creativity is the attribute of people to transform the world purposefully and consciously and carve out their own destiny. Underpinning the independence and creativity properties is consciousness, the property which enables people to recognise the characteristics of their surroundings and analyse the conditions for changing and developing them in accordance with their essential demands to live an independent and creative life.

The proposition that 'people are masters of everything and decide everything' is termed the philosophical principle of the Juche idea. The proposition that people are masters characterises the position of people in the world, and is rooted in the independence property. The proposition that people decide everything characterises the role of people in the world and is rooted in the creativity property. (In gaining familiarity with these terms and concepts, it is helpful to bear in mind the conceptual strings 'independence-position-mastery' and 'creativity-role-transformation'.) . . .

Besides its philosophical principle, the Juche idea puts forward socio-historical principles, which are based on the proposition that, unlike the natural world, the socio-historical movement has a subject, and that this subject is the people. Within this category it is the working class which most strongly aspires to independence and which consequently occupies the leading position in the struggle for social progress. . . .

Socialism and the World Today

The struggle of People's Korea to implement the guiding principles of the Juche idea has provided a body of experience that makes a unique contribution to the worldwide debate on how to build socialism, a contribution whose implications have significance beyond Korea alone.

In particular, the setbacks suffered by socialism during the past decade have failed to shake the conviction of Korea's revolutionaries in the superiority of socialism, and are seen as an example of the twists and turns that any new social system has had to face in its onward progress. Citing the fact that the first socialist state was established only eighty-one years ago, they compare the progress of socialism since then with the centuries-long and painful process of capitalism's replacement of the old order of feudalism. Indeed, bearing in mind the blockades, counter-revolutionary invasions and provocations which the socialist states have faced throughout their history, their record in building a new and better life for their people has in many cases been impressive indeed, as those in former socialist countries who now face restored capitalism have reason to recall. . . .

In rallying the world's people to resume their onward march towards a better future, People's Korea advances the concept of global independence. This concept, drawing on the lessons of the struggles of the past, calls for independent relations among the socialist countries, the invigoration of the Non-Aligned Movement and all other independent anti-imperialist forces, and the promotion of South-South trade and other forms of independent economic cooperation.

The greatest contribution any revolutionary movement can make to this cause of global independence is to achieve its own objectives. In Korea's case, these are to build socialism in the north, and to achieve the peaceful and independent reunification of their country, which will be an event that changes the face of the East Asian region and powerfully affects the balance of forces against imperialism and domination in the world as a whole.

People's Korea Faces the Future

In attempting to see People's Korea in the way the Koreans themselves see it, the recurring themes which constantly come to the fore are Korean reunification, the Juche idea, and the revolutionary leadership. These themes all flow together into one on the question of the succession of Kim Jong Il to the leadership of the Korean revolution.

This succession has been the culmination of a long process extending back to the early 1980s and even earlier. It carries with it the unmistakable message that the Juche idea, and with it the leadership method and style and indeed other every aspect of the thought and practice of Kim Il

Sung will be carried forward into the new generation, a generation that cannot fail to see further progress towards the country's reunification.

This succession process, which has culminated in Kim Jong Il assuming the highest offices of Party, state and army, has charted new territory in socialist theory and practice. For it is in the tempestuous struggles of anti-imperialist liberation war and the storms of socialist revolution that the majority of the most prestigious leaders of international socialism have won the hearts of their people; it was in fact the failure to sustain the unity and enthusiasm of these early stages of the struggle that led to the loss of revolutionary momentum in many of the former socialist countries. People's Korea has succeeded where those socialist states failed, with its people uniting around a leader of the new generation. The result is that the socialist system and its leadership retain the loyalty of the people, despite the setbacks to world socialism, despite catastrophic natural disasters, and despite the continuing imperialist blockade.

'Come hell, come high water', the Korean people will achieve their goals of defending and further developing their people-centred socialism and reuniting their divided country. Such, in the troubled world of 1998, is their unique message of determination and revolutionary optimism.

"Human rights are totally lacking in North Korea."

North Korea's Government Has Severely Oppressed Its People

International Human Rights League of Korea

Since 1948, the Democratic People's Republic of Korea (North Korea) has been ruled by two people: Kim Il Sung, who ruled from 1948 until his death in 1994, and Kim Jong Il, his son and designated successor. In the following viewpoint, the International Human Rights League of Korea contends that these two leaders have created an absolutist dictatorship that controls all aspects of the country's economic and political life and that significantly violates human rights. Many North Koreans languish in political prisons, and even those who are not imprisoned suffer from starvation. The IHRLK is a South Korea–based organization that works to publicize human rights abuses in North Korea.

As you read, consider the following questions:
1. What does the IHRLK assert about North Koreans' rights to free elections?
2. How many people are imprisoned in political prison camps, according to the authors?
3. What must the international community do in response to human rights abuses in North Korea, according to the IHRLK?

North Korean society can be depicted most vividly by quoting remarks made by Hans Meretzki, the last East German ambassador to Pyongyang. He said, "North Korea is an absolutist state decorated with socialism, or a dictatorial state which exercises an absolute right to command the people with Workers' Party and Juche Ideology as its background." He explained that the North Korean leadership has made all residents subject to a collective slavery by depriving them of individuality, and forcing them to engage in hard labor. Under these conditions, public life in North Korea is nothing but a continuation of military training.

Everyone has been deprived of human rights for a long time, and in this specific way, the regime has maintained total control.

Recently various international human rights organizations, including Amnesty International, the Freedom House and the U.S. State Department, have issued reports expressing significant worries about human rights violations in North Korea. These reports point out that the North Korean ruling hierarchy, in its effort to keep the populace under control, has been restricting the supply of food and clothing, as well as the freedom of residence, occupation, travel, press and assembly.

All North Korean citizens are divided into three classes, namely, the "core class" (20%), the "instable class" (45%), and the "hostile class" (27%). These classes are again divided into 51 sub-classes. Under this classification system, each citizen is given different food rations or medical service. One noteworthy fact is that the "hostile class" is under constant political surveillance. Members of this class are to be executed in an emergency case.

North Korea maintains no laws or regulations designed to protect human rights. The judicial authorities in North Korea are in fact tools of the Workers' Party, and therefore, the Party's policies or instructions are regarded more important than any laws. Kangaroo courts and public executions are held anywhere and at any time. Under these conditions, about 200,000 people have been confined in a dozen political prisoners' camps scattered throughout the country. These prisoners are suffering from various forms of human rights violations with little hope of being released from the camps.

The 49th U.N. Human Rights Subcommittee session on August 21, 1997, adopted a resolution calling upon North Korea to improve human rights conditions in the country and to abide by its obligation to submit human rights reports to the U.N. as stipulated by U.N. human rights regulations. The resolution also urged North Korea to take the necessary measures to guarantee freedom of movement and residence.

The human rights conditions in North Korea must no longer be regarded as minor problems in a specific country but as grave matters the international community must deal with.

Systematic Human Rights Violations

In North Korea, the instructions of Kim Il-sung or Kim Jong-il are regarded as the highest laws and even surpass the constitution or the decision of the Workers' Party. The North Korean constitution, in Article 11 stipulates, "the Democratic People's Republic of Korea carries out all its activities under the leadership of the Korean Workers' Party." But the Workers' Party charter, in the preamble, stipulates, "the Workers' Party is guided in its activities solely by the Great Leader Kim Il-sung's Juche ideology."

The constitution is a tool used to implement the instructions of Kim Il-sung which are designed to realize the collectivist principle. The constitution, in Article 63, stipulates, "in the Democratic People's Republic of Korea, the rights and duties of citizens are based on the collectivist principle of one for all and all for one." Under these conditions, individual human rights can be ignored.

The North Korean penal code is also designed to solidify the father-to-son hereditary dictatorship because it stipulates, "this code is designed to safeguard the Leader and his revolutionary line, thus to dye the whole society only with Juche Ideology" (Article 4). The penal code carries various articles designed to impose death and pecuniary punishment on all counter-revolutionary crimes which include the acts of slandering the "Leader" or resisting government policies (Articles 44–55, 105). The penal code denies the principle of "nulla poena sine lege," [no punishment without a law] and justifies retroactive punishment on the pretext that struggles against anti-social crimes must be escalated. The code also maintains clauses designed to punish not only criminals themselves but also their family members or relatives.

The Courts and prosecutors' offices also function to implement the instructions of the Leader and the Party. All North Korean laws are designed to force the people to unconditionally obey orders of Kim Il-sung and Kim Jong-il as well as Party policies. The laws have nothing to do with human rights.

Political Human Rights Abuses

By constitution (1992), all North Korean citizens are permitted to enjoy the right to elect and be elected (Article 66), and the freedom of speech, publishing, and assembly (Article 67). However, the reality is that rights and freedom are restricted by the policies designed to strengthen the "proletarian dictatorship."

North Korea conducts general elections to elect members of the Supreme People's Assembly (North Korean version of parliament), but the election is merely a formality to give the outside world the impression that the country maintains a democratic system. In fact, the election is designed to perpetuate the one-Party system because only one candidate is nominated by the Party for each electoral district, and voters are asked to cast only "aye" or "no" votes. As a result, elections always have 100% voter turn-out with 100% "aye" votes. The election on July 26 this year for example resulted in 99.87% voter turn-out with 100% "ayes", according to a North Korean announcement.

Voters have no choice but to cast an "aye" vote because Party officials are watching. If anyone abstains from voting, or votes "no", then he or she will be branded a counter-revolutionary and sent to one of the political prisoners' camps.

The North Korean press performs the function of propagating the Party's policies. The press never publishes any articles which may reflect negatively on the North Korean political system. All publications in North Korea are placed under the strict control and censorship of the Party. They praise the achievements of Kim Il-sung and Kim Jong-il, and support the Party policies.

North Korea operates various organizations to conduct political surveillance. The Workers' Party, the State Security Agency, and the Public Security Ministry (police) are the main organizations endowed with such functions. The State Security Agency is the secret police, and has agents planted in every workshop and village. Besides these organizations, North Korea operates the "5 household system," a political watch system comprising 5 households in every village. In this system, every member is used as an informant against every other member.

Economic Human Rights Abuses

The North Korean constitution stipulates, "the means of production are owned solely by the state and cooperative organizations" (Article 20), and "there is no limit to the properties that the state may own" (Article 21). As stipulated by the constitution, all public facilities as well as all factories, companies, banks, and all transportation means belong to the state. Private ownership is permitted only for some movable property possessed by an individual for personal use.

North Korean propaganda says that the people in North Korea are exempt from paying taxes. But the reality is that the state, as the sole owner of all production means, owns all products, and supplies the people, or employees, with minimum allowances, of food and clothing in the form of ration. In fact, the government is exploiting the people.

The food ration per person is decided in accordance with his or her social standing and job. Each ordinary citizen is to receive 700 grams of grain per day according to the official standard. But North Korea, due to aggravated economic conditions, has suspended the grain ration since 1995. Members of the elite group however still enjoy sufficient food. Currently most North Koreans are compelled to seek necessary food grains on the black market.

People in North Korea have been suffering from food shortages for several consecutive years; it is reported that more than a million people have died from starvation over the past 2 or 3 years. Starvation is one of the main reasons for a recent rise in the number of defectors from North Korea. Although the inefficient socialist economic system in

North Korea is responsible for the current economic crisis, the ruling hierarchy in Pyongyang persist in sticking with the inefficient system. This act of driving the people into starvation must be regarded as the most significant form of human rights violation.

Personality Cult Worship of the Leader

The late Kim Il-sung, in his effort to consolidate his position as a dictatorial leader, concentrated on a personality cult. North Korean propagandists fabricated various stories to enhance Kim's achievements; they constructed "revolutionary war sites" in 7 places, and "historical sites" in 34 places. The entire populace is mobilized by turns to participate in marches to these sites. In addition to these sites, they conduct "Classes to Study Kim Il-sung's Revolutionary Ideology" throughout the country to indoctrinate the people with the greatness of Kim Il-sung.

Various monuments are scattered throughout the country; they include 70 bronze statues of Kim Il-sung, 40,000 half-length plaster figures of Kim Il-sung, 250 monuments in praise of Kim Il-sung's achievements, 350 memorial halls, and 3,500 "towers of eternal life." In addition, all citizens are required to wear Kim Il-sung badges when they go out, and to hang pictures of Kim Il-sung and Kim Jong-il on the wall of the main room in their houses. . . .

Since the death of Kim Il-sung, North Korea has spent $94 million to stage various political events, $530 million to erect various monuments, $270 million to operate various propaganda facilities. North Korea watchers around the world estimate that North Korea has been spending at least $890 million annually to stage personality cult campaigns.

North Korea still holds events to celebrate Kim Il-sung's birthday anniversary (April 15) every year. For example, they stage mass games participated in by 50,000–100,000 students, and hold mass rallies and night soirees. North Korea is reportedly spending $23 million every year to invite 500–600 art troupe members from abroad to attend these occasions. . . .

Kim Jong-il, son of and successor to Kim Il-sung, has been steering all these personality cult projects. He has been trying to justify the hereditary succession of power by insisting, "revolutionary tasks must be carried out generation after generation." He has embalmed the body of his father, and has been trying to implant in the minds of the people the belief that Kim Il-sung is an eternal being. North Korea, in terminating a three year mourning period for Kim Il-sung in July 1997, declared that it had decided to use "Juche" as its calendar, instead of the current A.D. It designated 1912, the year of Kim Il-sung's birth, as the "first year of Juche," and April 15, the day of Kim Il-sung's birth, as the "Day of the Sun." This means that North Korea decided to worship Kim Il-sung as "God," or the "Sun," and as the "founder of the Juche Dynasty."

The Last Stalinist Regime

North Korea is the world's last true Stalinist regime. In most of the world, communism is dead, at least in everything but name. But in North Korea, totalitarian controls and a bizarre ideology have survived the collapse of the Soviet Union, the global wave of democratization and liberalization, the political transformation of South Korea, and the death in 1994 of dictator Kim Il Sung. Like almost everything else about the country, its very name—the "Democratic People's Republic of Korea"—is a grotesque, Orwellian lie.

Human rights reports from the State Department, Amnesty International, and elsewhere portray a regime so paranoid and ruthless that capital punishment is prescribed for such petty offenses as slandering the Communist Party, attempting to defect, listening to foreign broadcasts, or writing "reactionary" letters. The domineering regime forbids the sale or ownership of any radio that is not preset to receive only North Korean channels. The North Korean government, obsessed with power, spends a quarter of its gross domestic product on its military. And it is the systemic irrationality and cruelty of the North Korean system, much more than the vagaries of weather, that account for the country's current dreadful famine, in which hundreds of thousands are starving to death or have already perished.

Larry Diamond, *Hoover Digest*, no. 4, 1998.

Kim Jong-il now has luxurious villas in 32 places throughout the country. He has spent $2.5 billion to construct them.

Kim Jong-il's birthday is also observed as a national holiday in North Korea. . . .

Political Prisoners' Camps

The political prisoners' camps in North Korea are typically places where the worst human rights violations occur. The North Korean authorities officially call these camps "Management Centers." The people in the North use, "place of exile," "special dictatorship target area," or "political prisoners' concentration camps" when referring to these prisons.

According to a North Korean document captured by the U.S. army during the 1950–53 Korean War, North Korea began to operate the political prisoners' camps in 1947. In August, 1956, the North Korean hierarchy began to expand these camps when a mass political purge took place.

Through a residents registration program from 1967 to 1970, the North Korean authorities divided the populace into three classes, the "core class", the "instable class", and the "hostile class." Upon completing this program, the North Korean ruling hierarchy, based on the Cabinet Decision No. 149, conducted a large-scale purge of the "hostile class," 6,000 people were executed and a further 70,000 were imprisoned in the "No. 149 Target Area." Among the 70,000 prisoners, those who were branded anti-Party and anti–Kim Il-sung elements were relocated to the "special dictatorship target area," or political prisoners' camp.

Following the 6th Party Congress in 1980, when Kim Jong-il was officially nominated the successor to Kim Il-sung, about 15,000 persons, who were opposed to the hereditary succession plan, were arrested and sent to political prisoners' camps. Currently North Korea maintains a dozen camps of this kind in such areas as Kaechon (South Pyongan Province), Yodok (South Hamgyong Province), Hoeryong (North Hamgyong Province) and Chongjin. About 200,000 prisoners of conscience are detained in these camps.

Inmates of these political prisoners' camps are denied their basic rights, and routinely suffer from all forms of human rights violations including 12 hours of hard labor every day. The miserable conditions in these camps can be compared to those in the gulag operated by the Stalinist Soviet Union. . . .

The Status of Handicapped Persons

Foreigners will never see any handicapped people in Pyongyang or other big cities. This is because the North Korean authorities have removed them from public sight and resettled them in remote areas. Li Soon-ok, a woman who once had been an inmate in a North Korean prison and defected to the Republic of Korea in December 1995, revealed that the North launched the program to confine the handicapped in remote areas in the 1980s.

Other defectors from the North also say that in the 1980s the Pyongyang authorities ordered all handicapped persons, such as blind and deaf persons, hunchbacks, and mental patients to move, with their families from Pyongyang to remote places. Pyongyang in July 1989, prior to the holding of the 13th World Festival of Youth and Students, again took strict action to remove all handicapped persons from the city. It is said that they were confined on an isolated island off the west coast, or in such areas as Uchon in South Hamgyong Province, or Uiju in North Pyongan Province.

In the 1990s the North began to enforce the programs to remove handicapped persons who were in other cities, such as Nampo, Kaesong, and Chongjin, which were open to foreigners. North Korea has built special villages in remote areas in Uhrang County in Yanggan Province, and Chongsong County in North Hamgyong Province, to confine only dwarfs. They are confined there surrounded by double-stranded barbed wire fences. They are forbidden to contact ordinary people in the outside world. They are also forbidden to marry or to give birth to a child.

Defectors from the North

The number of defectors from the North began to rise in the 1990s when the socialist camp began to collapse. The number of defectors continues to increase due to the terrible food shortage.

Most North Koreans cross the northern border to reach China or Russia, but the defectors must elude the pursuit of North Korean agents. Only a few of them are successful in reaching the Republic of Korea.

It is reported that Kim Jong-il has ordered the arrest of all those who attempt to flee the country, saying, "to prevent a person from defecting is more important than capturing an espionage agent." On the orders of Kim Jong-il, North Korea newly organized a border guard unit under the name of the 10th Corps, and reinforced the border control capabilities by building mine fields along vulnerable points. The North Korean authorities also organized task force teams and dispatched them to China and Russia to arrest the successful defectors.

The defectors, once caught by these task force teams, are branded anti-state criminals, and dragged back to North Korea gagged and with a wire leash through their noses, to be publicly executed or to be confined in one of the political prisoners' camps in the North.

The Russian security authority in the Far East in May 1996 confirmed that one defector from North Korea whom the authority had handed over to the North Korean side was executed as soon as he reached the North.

No Human Rights in North Korea

Human rights are the universal values that all human beings, regardless of their nationality, race, religion or ideological differences, must enjoy. Unfortunately, such things as human rights are totally lacking in North Korea. Only revolutionary tasks and norms spurring the people to offer absolute loyalty to their leader exist in North Korea.

Under these norms, many innocent people have been confined in political prisoners' camps after being branded counter-revolutionaries. Moreover, most North Koreans have been suffering from starvation for several consecutive years.

The North Korean ruling hierarchy denies the values of liberal democracy and individualism, branding them evils; instead it urges the people to abide by the principles of collectivism and the North Korean form of socialism which are designed to prolong the existing dictatorship descending from father Kim to son Kim.

The human rights conditions in North Korea can only be improved when all the governments of the world, international human right organizations, and NGOs [nongovernmental organizations] join together in vigorous efforts to press the North Korean authorities to suspend their anti-human activities. North Korea insists that it has its own style of human rights, but the international community must consider the North's human rights violations as a most significant issue to be solved. The urgent task of the international community is to continue to press Pyongyang to accept universal values regarding human rights and open its doors to international human rights monitors.

Periodical Bibliography

The following articles have been selected to supplement the diverse views presented in this chapter.

Catherine Edwards   "How North Korea Starves Its People," *Insight on the News*, July 2, 2001.

Myung-Ha Eoh   "Democratic Citizenship Education in Korea," *Social Studies*, November 1999.

Christopher Hitchens   "Why North Korea Is Number One," *Newsweek*, July 9, 2001.

Kim Young Sam   "At Long Last: The Struggle for Democracy in Korea," *Harvard International Review*, Summer 1997.

Donald Kirk   "South Korea's New Activists," *New Leader*, March 2000.

Al Lance   "A Victory of Freedom in Korea," *American Legion Magazine*, September 2000.

Lee Min Bok   "Human Rights in North Korea," *Korea Focus*, May/June 2001.

Sejin Park   "Two Forces of Democratisation in Korea," *Journal of Contemporary Asia*, March 1998.

Jeff M. Sellers   "Forgotten Gulag," *Christianity Today*, August 6, 2001.

David I. Steinberg   "Korea: Triumph Amid Turmoil," *Journal of Democracy*, April 1998.

Time   "Out of the North Korean Gulag," July 9, 2001.

Young-Kwan Yoon   "South Korea in 1999," *Asian Survey*, January 2000.

James Zumwalt   "Seoul Chills Media, Clouding Democracy," *Washington Times*, August 26, 2001.

CHAPTER 3

What Should U.S. Foreign Policy Be Toward North and South Korea?

Chapter Preface

The United States has approximately thirty-seven thousand soldiers in South Korea—one of its largest standing deployments. Whether or not to withdraw these soldiers is one of the central debates regarding U.S. foreign policy in Asia.

The soldiers are a legacy of the Korean War, which was a surrogate battlefield of the cold war between the United States and the Soviet Union. Following World War II, Korea, which had been a Japanese colony, was divided along the 38th parallel into Soviet and American occupation zones. The temporary division of Korea became permanent when the former World War II allies could not agree on who would control a united Korea. This disagreement resulted in the creation of the Communist Democratic People's Republic of Korea (DPRK) in the north, backed by the Soviet Union, and the Republic of Korea (ROK) in the south, backed by the United States. Both the DPRK and the ROK claimed control over all of Korea.

In 1950, North Korean troops, trained and equipped by the Soviet Union, invaded South Korea and quickly overran much of the country. The United States had already withdrawn its troops from South Korea, and U.S. government officials had indicated that the Korean peninsula lay outside the main U.S. defense line in Asia. However, President Harry S. Truman, worried that a Communist takeover of Korea would give the Soviet Union a strategic advantage in the Cold War, quickly ordered naval, air, and ground forces to defend South Korea. After three years of fighting and 2 million battlefield fatalities (including thirty-three thousand Americans), North Korea and South Korea signed an armistice agreement. However, the two sides could not settle on a permanent peace treaty and remain technically in a state of war.

In the following decades, the place of the two Koreas in U.S. foreign policy was clear. As the Cold War persisted, South Korea was a vital anti-Communist ally, while North Korea was one of America's Communist foes. South Korea received economic assistance from the United States as well as U.S. troops on its soil and an American pledge to defend it against Communist aggression. Meanwhile, U.S.–North Korean relations ranged from strained to openly hostile. North Korea criticized American imperialism, while the United States criticized North Korea's record on human rights, its sponsorship of terrorism, and its military buildup on its border with South Korea. Despite the end of the Cold War, the American troops stationed in South Korea remain a stumbling block to any talk of normalizing diplomatic relations with North Korea.

While North Korea has long been an opponent of U.S. troops in South Korea, its calls for the troops' withdrawal have been joined by other voices. Some South Koreans have objected to their presence, arguing that they violate South Korean sovereignty and prevent a peaceful settlement between North and South Korea. Some American critics of U.S. policy argue that because South Korea has made great strides in economic and technological development, it is no longer as vulnerable to its impoverished northern neighbor. Furthermore, the strategic justification for intervening to defend South Korea in the first place—to prevent Soviet and Chinese gains in the Cold War—has vanished with the end of the Cold War. "A war between North and South Korea would be just that—a war between North and South Korea," asserts analyst Doug Bandow. "The obvious humanitarian tragedy would generate few security concerns for the U.S."

However, many analysts strongly defend the presence of U.S. troops in South Korea. They argue that South Korea remains a valuable U.S. ally in Asia—and one that is vulnerable to possible North Korean invasion. In addition, many believe a withdrawal of U.S. troops in Korea would threaten both regional stability and U.S. interests. "The future of Asia will importantly depend on what happens to American forces now stationed along the 38th parallel," asserts former Secretary of State Henry Kissinger. The following viewpoints debate the place of American soldiers in Korea and other urgent issues confronting U.S. foreign policy makers.

> *"Washington should phase out its troop presence and security guarantees. South Korea is well able to defend itself."*

The United States Should Withdraw from South Korea

Doug Bandow

Since an armistice in 1953 ended the Korean War, the United States has stationed troops in South Korea and has pledged to come to its defense in the event of North Korean attack. In the following viewpoint, Doug Bandow argues that American foreign policy regarding South Korea should be rethought and American soldiers there withdrawn. Circumstances have changed, he argues, most notably the end of the Cold War between the United States and North Korea's Communist supporters, the Soviet Union and China. It is time, he believes, for the Republic of (South) Korea to take more responsibility for its own defense. Bandow is a senior fellow at the Cato Institute and the author of *Tripwire: Korea and U.S. Foreign Policy in a Changed World*.

As you read, consider the following questions:
1. Why does Bandow consider Korea to be such a dangerous situation for the United States?
2. Why did President Harry S. Truman intervene in Korea in 1950, according to the author?
3. What policy recommendations does Bandow make concerning North Korea?

The planned [June 2000] summit between South Korean President Kim Dae-jung . . . and . . . North Korean leader Kim Jong-il offers the hope of ending the Korean Peninsula's Cold War. Washington should use this opportunity to reduce its involvement in Korean affairs.

A Dangerous Military Commitment

Korea has for 50 years been one of America's most dangerous military commitments. Today the United States maintains 37,000 soldiers as a tripwire to ensure involvement should war again break out between the two Koreas.

Indeed, there is no place else in the world where Americans are more likely to be involved in a conflict. The United States would win any war, but it would not be a bloodless victory. . . .

Yet, the Korean Peninsula is not nearly as important as American policy suggests. Neither the Pentagon nor Gen. Douglas MacArthur [who commanded American forces during much of the Korean War] believed South Korea to be intrinsically significant in 1950. President Harry S. Truman intervened to stop North Korea's invasion because he believed it was inspired by the Soviet Union.

We now know that the Soviets were reluctant supporters of Pyongyang's offensive. In any case, the Soviet Union is gone, along with any threat of global conquest.

A Peripheral Interest

Thus, by any definition, Korea today is a peripheral rather than a vital U.S. interest. War there would be tragic, but would not threaten America.

Moreover, the Republic of Korea need no longer play the role of helpless victim. The South has won the competition between the two Koreas.

It has 30 times the gross domestic product (GDP), twice the population, and a vast technological lead. South Korea, in contrast to the North, is a major international player.

Indeed, Russia is shipping weapons to South Korea to pay off its debts. China, too, is unlikely to back Pyongyang in any war.

Obviously, North Korea remains a dangerous actor. But

its threats are largely empty—desperate attempts to gain international attention. Bankrupt, starving, and friendless, the North is struggling to survive, not to dominate South Korea, let alone the region.

Questioning America's Military Presence

The Pentagon maintains that the security alliance between the United States and the Republic of Korea (South Korea) "serves as the foundation on which all U.S. diplomatic, defense and economic efforts on the Korean peninsula rest." However, South Korea, while officially still at war with its northern counterpart, has found it increasingly burdensome to maintain the 37,000 U.S. troops and nearly 100 U.S. military installations on the peninsula. U.S. personnel in South Korea have been responsible for sexual exploitation and violence, as well as thousands of unrecognized and disadvantaged Amerasian children. Prostitution serving the U.S. military in South Korea is pervasive. According to a study by the women's organization Sae Woom Tuh, an estimated 20,000 women work in the bars of the *kijichon*, or U.S. military camp towns. They earn an average of U.S.$170 per month, are forced to work in deplorable conditions and receive one day off each month.

The high number and heinous nature of crimes committed against bar women by U.S. personnel have galvanized Korean citizens against the U.S. military presence. The National Campaign for the Eradication of Crime by U.S. Troops in Korea was formed in 1992 after the brutal murder and mutilation of a bar woman, Yoon Geum Yi. Her murderer, Kenneth Markle, was convicted and sentenced in a Korean court only after massive citizen protests forced the U.S. Army to surrender jurisdiction. According to a parliamentary inquiry, from January 1993 to June 1996 nearly 2,300 crimes were committed by U.S. military personnel against Korean citizens. The National Campaign's statistics show that of the 2,730 crimes attributed to U.S. personnel in 1991–1992, only 31 suspects, 1.1%, were ever prosecuted.

Rachel Cornwell and Andrew Wells, *Peace Review*, September 1999.

Even its most worrisome activities, such as missile and nuclear weapons research, look more like strategies to defend itself in an increasingly hostile world than to prepare itself for an aggressive war. When your neighboring enemy spends as much on defense as your entire GDP, and is allied with the world's greatest military power, you don't have many defense options.

The Summit Surprise

The summit announcement is one of the most dramatic developments on a peninsula long noted for surprises. Six years ago [in 1994], Kim Jong-il's father, Kim Il-sung, was set to meet Kim Dae-jung's predecessor, Kim Young-sam. Kim Il-sung dropped dead shortly before the meeting, however, and relations between the two nations quickly deteriorated.

Since that time, North Korea has suffered famine, near economic collapse and, if reports are accurate, political infighting. The only card Pyongyang has had to play to gain international attention and assistance is the threat to misbehave.

Kim Jong-il's apparent willingness to meet with Kim Dae-jung is another sign of desperation. Even if the meeting falls through, Pyongyang has conceded the legitimacy of its southern counterpart.

Of course, a successful summit is not sufficient to end a half-century of hostilities. The North has initiated war, regularly employed terrorism, launched frequent military probes, and constantly rattled its saber. Seoul has returned the hostile feelings, if not actions.

But a meeting of the two Kims would provide an opportunity for their two nations to start anew. Moreover, it would offer Washington a chance to step into the background.

America Should Step Aside

The United States should leave the direction of Korean policy to Seoul. The country most threatened by North Korea is South Korea. The country with the most to gain from detente between the two is South Korea.

America should normalize its relationship with both countries. For the North, that means dropping economic sanctions and initiating diplomatic relations.

Of course, such a policy would "reward" Pyongyang, but that is precisely what the United States should do when North Korea acts responsibly. Such an opening may not be enough to defang what remains a militarized yet unpredictable regime, but it is more likely to have positive results than is the current policy.

As for the South, Washington should phase out its troop presence and security guarantees. South Korea is well able to defend itself. The justification for an American tripwire disappeared long ago.

The Korean Peninsula is entering an exciting new era. The two Koreas may be finally willing to put their 50-year old struggle behind them.

In any case, it is time for Washington to disengage. Then South Korea and its neighbors, rather than America, are the ones that have to deal with future bumps in the Korean road to peace and reunification.

> "Hasty withdrawal of United States Forces in Korea (USFK) could put Korea's long-term security at risk."

The United States Should Not Withdraw from South Korea

Glenn Baek

Since a 1953 armistice ended hostilities in the Korean War, the United States has maintained a significant number of U.S. soldiers in South Korea. Many South Koreans and some Americans have questioned the rationale for the continuing American military presence. In the following viewpoint, Glenn Baek acknowledges the existence of antitroop sentiment in South Korea, but argues that the presence of American soldiers remains necessary to protect South Korea from possible North Korean attack as well as to preserve peace and stability in the region. Baek is a research associate in the International Security Program at the Center for Strategic and International Studies (CSIS), a research foundation based in Washington, D.C.

As you read, consider the following questions:
1. What has motivated South Korean opposition to U.S. troops, according to Baek?
2. What harms might occur from U.S. withdrawal from South Korea, in the author's view?
3. What recommendations does Baek make to the governments of South Korea and the United States?

A s Koreans commemorate the 50th anniversary of the Korean War and anticipate the beginning of a North-South reconciliation after the first-ever summit [between leaders of North and South Korea], they are openly questioning the rationale of long-term U.S. troop presence on their soil. This growing trend contravenes shifting U.S. policy priorities from Western Europe to the Asia-Pacific region in light of the looming political-military challenge posed by China. More importantly, growing local opposition to continued U.S. troop presence in Korea could undermine Washington's vital security role in the region and ultimately put Korea's long-term security in peril.

South Korean Grievances

This anti-U.S.-troop sentiment is highlighted by the Nogun-ri allegations [involving the mass killings of Korean civilians in 1950, allegedly by U.S. troops, at the village of Nogun-ri], a training accident involving U.S. aircraft [in which bombs were accidentally dropped near a small village in May 2000], and the renewal of long-standing legal disputes involving U.S. troops. Although investigations into the alleged massacre of Korean civilians by U.S. troops at Nogun-ri revealed a number of discrepancies in the evidence, the widely publicized story has already fueled simmering public resentment toward the United States. Furthermore, the collateral damage to a Korean village caused by a malfunctioning U.S. fighter plane has highlighted frustration over the cost of hosting foreign troops. Other grievances range from environmental degradation near U.S. military training grounds to the payment of host-nation support for the U.S. bases.

However, no other issue stirs the feelings of Koreans more than the notion of "unequal" partnership reflected in the Status of Forces Agreement (SOFA), a legal document that governs the rights of 37,000 U.S. troops in Korea. Many Koreans believe that their nation's limited jurisdiction over U.S. soldiers arrested for committing crimes against Koreans is a national insult and that the Agreement needs to be revised. The public becomes particularly bitter in cases involving the murder of Korean barmaids by U.S. servicemen. This tragic occurrence has attracted extensive local media coverage and has both undermined support for U.S. troop presence and ignited the movement for SOFA revision.

Most Koreans Want Americans to Stay

Despite the growing anti-Americanism among Korean youths, an absolute majority of Koreans are still thankful for the Americans' coming to their rescue during the 1950 communist invasion, sacrificing over 50,000 of their soldiers' lives.

They also approve the continuing U.S. forces presence on the southern half of the Korean peninsula, believing that the United States Forces in Korea (USFK), in alliance with Republic of Korea (ROK) armed forces, is the main bulwark that deters belligerent North Korea from daring to launch another full-scale invasion.

Korea Times, October 13, 1999.

These events, coupled with growing frustration and discontent among Koreans, have given ample ammunition to powerful civic groups bent on swaying public opinion against U.S. troop presence. The anti-U.S.-troop sentiment cuts across the generation-divide, attracting younger Koreans despite their allegiance to American pop culture. Furthermore, the movement appears to be enjoying subtle endorsement by the Korean government. Stopping short of lending official support, the Kim Dae-jung administration has launched speedy investigations into training accidents and is persistently calling for the revision of SOFA. Gone are the days when public resentment toward the United States was either simply dismissed or suppressed.

The Risks of U.S. Troop Withdrawal

Today's vocal anti-U.S.-troop sentiment reflects Korea's maturing democratization and its aspiration to be treated as an "equal" in the eyes of the United States. Indeed, Korea has come a long way since the devastating aftermath of its internecine war and decades of authoritarian rule. However, hasty withdrawal of United States Forces in Korea (USFK) could put Korea's long-term security at risk. North Korea remains an unpredictable state capable of great destructive power, and competing geostrategic interests in the region could easily engulf Korea into an unwanted conflict in the absence of USFK. For the United States, troop withdrawal would considerably diminish its role and influence not only on the Korean peninsula but throughout Asia.

Although the changing nature of the Korean political landscape forces USFK and its host to reevaluate their role and relationship, it is in both their interests to maintain U.S. troops to ensure stability on the peninsula and the region. Meanwhile, the two governments must launch a far-reaching public information campaign explaining the utility of continued troop presence and the immense resources required to maintain readiness to defend against the North Korean threat. Equally, they must elevate the SOFA revision talks to a higher political level in order to reach a swift, mutually satisfying outcome.

At a time when the prospects for peace on the Korean peninsula have never been greater, the very presence that helped to sustain a fragile peace has now become a contentious issue that could unravel the achievements of the U.S.-Korea alliance and threaten their long-term security interests. How the two countries resolve their problems today will ultimately shape the future of U.S. troop presence in Korea beyond any North-South reconciliation.

"An approach based on incentives and cooperation might work with North Korea."

The United States Should Engage with North Korea

David Wright

Some analysts have argued that the United States should isolate and weaken the "outlaw" North Korean regime in the hopes of forcing either its reform or its collapse. In the following viewpoint, David Wright argues that a collapse of the North Korean government would be a dangerous development. A better foreign policy approach would be to engage with North Korea politically and economically in order to induce it to cooperate more with other nations. He analyzes the 1994 Agreed Framework between North Korea and the United States, in which North Korea agreed to limits on its nuclear weapons program in exchange for foreign assistance in building two commercial nuclear power facilities. He argues that the arrangement, while not perfect, has achieved its main goals of preventing further nuclear proliferation. The United States should explore more avenues of potential cooperation with North Korea, he concludes. Wright is a senior staff scientist at the Union of Concerned Scientists, an organization concerned with environmental and nuclear issues.

As you read, consider the following questions:
1. What actions of North Korea have made it seem to be a threatening "outlaw" state, according to Wright?
2. According to Wright, what kinds of economic aid might be part of an incentive package for North Korea?

In the past decade, North Korea has made headlines and gained the reputation of being an "outlaw" state. In particular, reports of its programs to develop nuclear weapons and ballistic missiles have caused international concern.

In the early 1990s, evidence surfaced that North Korea was secretly producing weapons-grade plutonium. Tensions between the United States and North Korea over the nuclear issue nearly erupted into war in the spring of 1994. A negotiated settlement—the Agreed Framework of October 1994—stopped the plutonium production and tamed the war talk, but remains controversial in the United States.

In the 1980s North Korea began to build copies of the Soviet Scud-B missile, which had a range of about 300 kilometers, along with an improved version with a 500-kilometer range. It sold hundreds of these missiles to states in the Middle East, especially Iran and Syria.

In 1993, North Korea tested a new missile, the Nodong, with a reported range of 1,000–1,300 kilometers with a one-ton payload, which it apparently sold to Pakistan. It also has reportedly helped Iran develop a similar missile.

And in August 1998, it tested a three-stage missile, the Taepodong-1, that carried a small payload several thousand kilometers. Conducting the test over Japan without notification struck almost everyone as provocative.

Moreover, North Korea's bombastic and threatening rhetoric toward the outside world and its history of sending miniature submarines and spies into South Korean territory have compounded concerns about its hostile intentions. Further, North Korea remains a closed society, and the outside world has a poor understanding of its policy-making process.

The good news is that the United States may be able to play a significant role in reducing this threat if it chooses to, since North Korea seems to see its relationship with the United States as pivotal.

Containment or Engagement?

What, then, should the United States do?

Some argue that the United States should increase North Korea's political and economic isolation in an attempt to further weaken the country and either force reform or hasten collapse of the current regime. In the meantime, the United States would plan to deter or if necessary repel any military attacks by North Korea.

Proponents of this approach maintain it would be effective since they believe, with the end of massive aid following the split-up of the Soviet Union, North Korea is on the brink of collapse. Indeed, its economy is in desperate straits, declining by more than five percent a year since the early 1990s and famine is widespread.

The considerable support in the United States for this approach grows out of the bitter history between the two countries and the continuing military threat that North Korea poses on the Korean peninsula. The United States and North Korea do not have diplomatic relations and formally remain in a state of war because no treaty ended the Korean War. The United States keeps 37,000 troops, and until recently nuclear weapons, in South Korea. Since the late 1980s, the United States has designated North Korea as a "terrorist country," and has imposed economic sanctions that prohibit essentially all trade between the countries, except for humanitarian aid.

Moreover, it is commonly believed in the United States that North Korea's leaders see increased military strength as vital to their survival. And they are seen to be reckless, unpredictable, and perhaps irrational. How then could anyone expect to deal with them in other ways?

Shortcomings of Containment

But this approach has serious shortcomings. Despite the failing economy, the North Korean regime appears capable of limping along for a long time. Further steps by the West to isolate North Korea or threaten it militarily may actually strengthen the hand of hardliners in North Korea and push its policy in exactly the wrong direction.

And collapse carries severe risks. North Korea's neighbors worry about floods of post-collapse refugees. And they worry even more about the possibility that a regime pushed to the brink might strike out militarily in its death throes.

An alternate approach is to try to engage North Korea politically and economically, to create incentives for it to cooperate with the international community. The goal would be to reduce the military threat North Korea poses, not just deter and contain it, and to do so in a cooperative, verified way.

Indeed, the economic crisis and famine may make North Korea more receptive to carrots than sticks. Indeed, key North Korean officials may have come to believe that normalizing relations with the United States and dealing with North Korea's economy is more important for the long-term existence of the state than is its military power.

There is, of course, no guarantee that engagement would work. But despite North Korea's heated rhetoric and frustrating actions, there are intriguing signs that it might respond to this approach. It is an approach that policy-makers need to give a serious try.

There is now a window of opportunity to successfully engage North Korea with the Kim Dae-Jung government in South Korea. Kim has advocated engagement with the North, unlike the previous South Korean leaders, and he even asked the United States to ease sanctions when he addressed Congress in June 1998. But political support within South Korea for engagement could erode if no progress is made on improving relations.

The Agreed Framework

Perhaps the most important example of engagement with North Korea was the negotiation of the Agreed Framework of October 1994. This agreement remains controversial, largely because of the provision to build two nuclear power reactors in North Korea in return for the dismantling of North Korea's existing nuclear reactors. But North Korea agreed to stop production of weapons plutonium and has done so under verification at its Yongbyon nuclear facility. The United States says that it has no evidence of production at other sites.

The United States says it has no evidence of production at other sites, although construction at an underground site at Kumchang-ri that U.S. intelligence believes may be nuclear-related has added to the controversy. Talks to give the United States access to this site are making progress.

North Korean actions prior to signing the 1994 accord

may also be revealing. From 1992 to 1994, North Korea could have pulled fuel rods from its reactor and extracted weapons plutonium, but it did not. Some U.S. analysts and officials involved in the negotiations interpreted this apparent self-restraint as a sign of North Korea's interest in negotiating limits to its nuclear program.

This restraint—if that is what it was—as well as the signing of the Agreed Framework would be unlikely actions if a country's top priority was the acquisition of weapons of mass destruction. . . .

In addition, North Korea has taken a number of smaller but unprecedented steps in the past several years—such as allowing joint searches with the United States for the remains of soldiers from the Korean War—that suggest it is rethinking its relation to the rest of the world.

Incentives for Negotiation

North Korea presumably has a number of incentives for negotiating limits on its missile program.

A decade ago, missile sales reportedly brought North Korea significant income and supplies of oil from the Middle East, but this is apparently no longer true. Persistent reports that North Korea's sales of missiles and missile technology bring in upwards of $500 million annually appear to hark back to several years in the 1980s, when the Iran-Iraq war resulted in high demand for Scuds.

North Korea may now see that the greatest value of its missile program lies in its value to the United States and other countries in negotiations. Pyongyang undoubtedly sees its nuclear and missile programs as two of the few things it can use to bargain for an easing of sanctions and significant amounts of economic assistance.

Moreover, North Korean leaders presumably recognize that to improve relations with other countries in an attempt to improve its economy, they must reduce international concerns about North Korean weapons programs.

What Should the Goals of Talks Be?

As part of a threat-reduction package, the United States should seek a complete ban on the sale or transfer of technology for all ballistic and cruise missiles, as well as a ban on technical assistance for such systems.

History suggests that monitoring of missile transfers can be done reasonably well. Verifying an end to technical assistance will be more difficult, but it is important to build into any agreement clear prohibitions on these activities.

Why Engage with North Korea?

Why should the West and the other countries deal with such an unpredictable regime? The simple answer is that there is no sensible alternative. Engagement does not imply approval of the regime or its policies, merely a recognition that North Korea is an important part of North East Asia's security environment which we should not ignore. Isolating North Korea would increase, rather than diminish, the risk of instability in North East Asia and worsen the already atrocious living conditions of ordinary North Koreans.

While military confrontation between the two Koreas cannot be ruled out, the greater danger is that 'a disintegrating North Korea could precipitate a large exodus of refugees into neighbouring countries'. The sudden unravelling of the North Korean state is in no-one's interests. That is why the South Korean government has concluded rapprochement is preferable to confrontation or containment, a position that the US and several European states are now taking.

Sharif M. Shuja, *Contemporary Review*, December 2000.

Ultimately, in addition to ending missile transfers, the goal should be to stop future development of North Korean missiles and require the destruction of existing missiles and facilities for missile development and production, at least for missiles with ranges greater than a given threshold. A first step would be to negotiate a ban on the flight testing of missiles, which could be readily verified by U.S. satellites.

An agreement that banned further flight testing of missiles would, from a Western perspective, place a meaningful limit on the future development of North Korean missiles. It would leave the Taepodong-1 missile with a single flight test, and the longer-range Taepodong-2 with none.

A flight-test ban could be combined with other measures intended to restrict missile development, such as shutting down missile research and development facilities and banning ground tests needed to develop new engines. While satellite monitoring could help verify some of these activities, additional verification measures would have to be negotiated. . . .

A Credibility Gap

North Korea's credibility in abiding by its agreements is frequently questioned in the United States. But from North Korea's point of view, the Agreed Framework has led to a serious credibility problem for the United States as well.

North Korea has seen that many members of Congress are hostile to the agreement. As a result, the . . . [United States in 1999] is now in technical violation of the agreement since it is behind schedule in providing the heavy fuel oil the United States is obligated to supply, even though it represents only a relatively modest amount of money ($30–40 millions annually). Further, there have been repeated congressional calls for cutting all funding for the accord.

Moreover, North Korea apparently believed the Agreed Framework was the beginning of a process of engagement with the United States, and would lead to an easing of sanctions, which has not happened. It now sees the United States as interested only in capping North Korea's nuclear weapons program. Further, from the perspective of North Korea, the United States lacks the political will to significantly change the relationship between the two countries. This may be leading to North Korean cynicism about negotiations and about U.S. intentions or ability to deliver on future promises of political normalization and economic assistance.

Thus, North Korea may believe that without its ability to threaten, to make headlines, the prospects for U.S. engagement or assistance would remain small. Indeed, some of North Korea's actions may be directed at creating crises intended to refocus U.S. attention on diplomatic engagement. . . .

While there have been several meetings between U.S. and North Korean negotiators on North Korea's missile program, the United States has apparently not tried to put a broad package on the negotiating table. North Korea seems unwilling to negotiate in earnest on its missile program until it believes the United States is serious about constructive engagement on a wider scale.

The United States should put high-level political support behind a policy of engagement and put together a negotiating package that conveys to North Korea a commitment to the negotiating process. Only then can the United States begin to determine whether such an approach may work. . . .

The Package

The U.S. negotiating package should consist of a set of phased and linked measures that would create strong incentives for North Korea to abide by the terms of the agreement. . . .

A key part of the package would be political. According to experts on North Korea, such as Tony Namkung of the Atlantic Council, the North Korean desire to be treated with respect and to begin a process of normalizing relations with the United States is even greater than its desire for economic assistance. To be sure, it is also concerned about its economy and its ability to feed its people, and measures that would help in these areas would be needed in a negotiation package. But political normalization with the United States is the key issue that ultimately must be on the table. . . .

To emphasize the political aspects of the package, a high-level U.S. envoy . . . should travel to North Korea and declare a U.S. desire to end the era of adversarial relations. The United States should also declare its readiness to open a liaison office in Pyongyang and to have North Korea do so in the United States. (The latter step was expected to occur by the end of 1998, but the plan was scuttled by North Korea's missile launch in August.)

Beyond that, there are a number of measures that could be part of a package—although, given the present mood on Capitol Hill, measures that would require Congress to appropriate funds may be difficult to offer.

- Some amount of hard currency may be necessary for an agreement banning missile sales. North Korea has said that its "missile export is aimed at obtaining foreign currency"; to end exports, it said, the United States would have to lift its economic embargo "as early as possible" and compensate North Korea for its foregone sales. (North Korea is reportedly seeking $1 billion a year for three years.) . . .

Compensation, however, could take other forms, including some of those discussed below.

- The United States could waive all sanctions associated with the Trading With the Enemy Act (TWEA), an action the president can take. This would open U.S. markets to North Korean companies or companies doing business there. Easing sanctions would be an important sign of a U.S. commitment to the process of political and economic normalization.

  Further, dropping TWEA sanctions would be important even it if does not initially lead to a significant opening of direct U.S. trade and investment.

  It would allow the United States, for instance, to grant North Korea an annual textile quota and permit South Korean and other foreign investors now being courted by Pyongyang to export textiles and other products made with low-wage North Korean labor to the U.S. market. That would allow North Korea to earn foreign exchange and it could encourage further opening of North Korea to foreign investment.

- The United States could make a major contribution to the United Nations Development Program (UNDP) initiative intended to help North Korea grow more of its own food through measures such as the repair of irrigation systems, assistance with fertilizer, and the like. . . .

- The United States could also make a commitment to help North Korea improve its mining sector. Minerals are one of North Korea's main potential resources for foreign exchange. The United States could help establish a minerals development fund to assist North Korea in developing its mining technology and infrastructure. In turn, this might encourage private capital to help develop the mining sector.

A Pragmatic Approach

The experience with Iraq highlights the difficulties of trying to limit weapons development in an uncooperative state. Fortunately, there is evidence that an approach based on incentives and cooperation might work with North Korea. . . .

Ultimately, of course, the United States may conclude that a strategy of containment and isolation is the best it can do. But it makes no sense to start with such a strategy.

A hard-nosed, pragmatic approach to national security demands that the United States seriously pursue a policy of engagement with North Korea to find out if it will work.

| "*Despite the fact that we have in a one-sided way constantly offered North Korea opportunities to engage, they have not done so.*"

U.S. Engagement with North Korea Has Been a Failure

Christopher Cox

Christopher Cox is a conservative Republican member of Congress who was first elected in 1988. He was a member of a Republican group of Congress members (the North Korea Advisory Group) that in 1999 submitted a report critical of President Bill Clinton's policies on North Korea. The following viewpoint is taken from testimony Cox presented before the House Committee on International Relations in October 1999. He argues that although the United States is giving extensive foreign aid to North Korea, the nation's repressive regime has not adequately reciprocated by moderating its behavior. North Korea has not fully lived up to its promises under the 1994 Agreed Framework to freeze its nuclear program and negotiate with South Korea, he asserts. In addition, North Korea continues to provide missiles and missile technology to other nations and to engage in drug trafficking. Cox concludes that U.S. economic assistance to North Korea should be stopped.

As you read, consider the following questions:

1. According to Cox, what threatening actions has North Korea taken?
2. What should be the ultimate goal of the United States concerning North Korea's "Stalinist" government, according to Cox?

Excerpted from Christopher Cox's testimony before the Committee on International Relations, House of Representatives, One Hundred Sixth Congress, First Session, October 13, 1999.

In my view, U.S. policy is conducting a one-sided love affair with the regime in North Korea. But despite the fact that we have in a one-sided way constantly offered North Korea opportunities to engage, they have not done so.

We have made, we, the United States, specifically the Clinton Administration, have made North Korea the No. 1 recipient of U.S. foreign aid in the region. Now we are offering North Korea normal relations in return for their commitment to abide by paper promises, notwithstanding a recent history under the 1994 Agreed Framework of violated promises and a half century of truce talks and similar performance.

Furthermore, this is not without consequence to regional security. North Korea continues to threaten American and allied interests. You all know that on August 31st of last year [1998], North Korea launched a missile over Japan. But their disdain for human life was such that they refused even to give a mariner's warning to ships in the target area for the missile.

On December 8th last [1998], North Korea very publicly threatened "to blow up the entire territory of the United States." They pledged to do so even if it required arming its children with bombs and sending them on suicide missions.

North Korea has sold and continues to sell missiles and missile technology to unstable parts of the world where they could do the greatest harm. They provided crucial technology to Iran, as you know, for their Shahab missile that now threatens U.S. forces across the Middle East. To Pakistan they provided technology for the Ghauri missile that threatens the fragile stability of South Asia.

When American negotiators sought restraint from North Korea on the sale of these missiles, North Korea used the opportunity to demand one-half billion dollars in compensation. When North Korea was asked to reveal a potential nuclear site in the mountains of Kumchangri, one of many suspect sites that should be open to inspection under the terms of an existing agreement, the 1992 Agreement between North and South Korea, North Korea again demanded compensation.

North Korea continues to engage in counterfeiting and drug sales as a matter of national policy, in spite of what should be international embarrassment suffered by its diplomats and ship captains caught in these criminal activities. It is this repeated indication of callous disregard for world opinion, let alone American opinion, that should give us great caution and skepticism in [dealing with North Korea].

The 1994 Agreement

The final piece of evidence is the 1994 Agreed Framework and our experience under it. In 1994, the Clinton Administration signed an agreement with North Korea that it heralded then as ending North Korea's nuclear program and reversing the regime's dangerous isolation. We in Congress have given that agreement many years now to work and we have years of experience in watching how it worked and how that approach works.

The 1994 Agreed Framework sought an end to North Korea's nuclear program, but the Administration now admits that North Korea maintains its capabilities to process plutonium on a moment's notice. . . .

After this 1994 Agreed Framework was signed, the Administration described it as a complete freeze of North Korea's nuclear weapons development program. Now the Administration claims that it has shut down only two of North Korea's nuclear sites, and the nuclear weapons development program continues.

In the same 1994 Agreement, North Korea agreed to promote North-South talks. But it has thwarted every negotiation since then, even with Kim Dae Jung's conciliatory South Korean government. In 1999, North Korean ships, as you know, forced a confrontation with South Korean naval vessels in the Yellow Sea.

How North Korea has performed under this 1994 Agreed Framework is of great importance to what you are going to hear today, because if you cannot accept North Korea's promises, then even if they make the promises that we hope they will make in return for the concessions that we are anticipatorily granting, we will be left nowhere different than where we started.

Under the terms of this agreement, . . . the United States and its allies will only provide light-water reactors to North Korea if we and they are satisfied with North Korea's performance. As Secretary of Defense Dr. [William] Perry told us, when arguing on behalf of the agreement before the Senate Foreign Relations Committee, U.S. compliance with that agreement should be predicated on what they, North Korea, did step by step. So here we are, and we can take a look at what they did step by step.

"We're happy to announce that we've reached an agreement!"

Lurie's World. © 1994 by Cartoonews International Syndicate, N.Y.C., USA. Reprinted with permission.

It also matters because there are new threats that may develop as a result of the provision of these reactors to North Korea. The light-water reactors, for starters, cost about $5 billion, and this is a significant enrichment of the failing regime in Pyongyang. But more to the point, these reactors also pose the threat of increased nuclear proliferation because the light-water reactors can also be used to produce nuclear weapons-grade material for an expanding inventory of North Korean nuclear weapons.

These are the reasons for the U.S. to take a cautious and skeptical approach when we look at North Korea's duplicitous performance under the 1994 Agreed Framework. But the Administration's policy in response to North Korea's violations of the 1994 Agreed Framework has been systematically to reward North Korea for its most dangerous misconduct. Time has worked to Pyongyang's advantage, and will continue to do so as North Korea's military capabilities are allowed to improve.

So I would suggest to all of you that a new policy is very urgently needed now. A piece of that policy should be . . . to strengthen United States and allied defenses in the region. That should be given highest priority. But the KEDO [Korean Peninsula Energy Development Organization, an international organization established to carry out provisions of the 1994 Agreed Framework] nuclear appeasement has to end. . . .

KEDO funding . . . should be permanently ended, and furthermore, there ought to be no buy-off of North Korea's missile program so that additional suspect sites can be inspected. . . .

We don't have, at least I haven't seen from the [Clinton] Administration, a plan for regime change in North Korea. So what we are trying to do is introduce just new elements and see what happens. But the new elements we are introducing, private interests, will become a lobby in the United States for U.S. aid to North Korea, so that this desperately poor country will have some wherewithal to buy what it is they are selling. That cycle of lobbying then becomes pressure on Congress to do the wrong thing. It will supplant any kind of objective appraisal of what ought to be our security policy toward North Korea. . . .

North Korea hasn't any wherewithal to buy [materials] itself because it has a Stalinist Government. We ought to be focused on getting rid of that Stalinist Government, not sustaining it.

| *"The US needs to make a bold political decision to resolve this military stalemate of 50 years."*

The United States Should Make Peace with North Korea

Indong Oh

Indong Oh, a physician, is director of Korea-2000, a Los Angeles–based research council that explores avenues that could lead to Korean unification. In the following viewpoint, he argues that the United States should break the military and political stalemate in the Korean peninsula by signing a peace agreement with North Korea and by gradually withdrawing its forces from South Korea. Such actions would reduce South Korea's dependence on the United States and assuage North Korean fears of American intentions in the region. The ultimate goal of U.S. policy should be a peacefully reunited and nuclear-free Korea, he concludes.

As you read, consider the following questions:

1. What motivates North Korea's nuclear weapons program, according to Oh?
2. Why is the United States in a better position than North Korea to take diplomatic risks without jeopardizing its national security, in the author's opinion?
3. How has the democratization of South Korea changed the prospects of peace between the two Koreas, according to Oh?

Excerpted from "Time to Commit to Peace Regime in the Korean Peninsula," by Indong Oh, *Northeast Asia Peace and Security Network Special Report*, ftp.nautilus.org, June 8, 2000. Copyright © 2000 by the Nautilus Institute. Reprinted by permission of the publisher and the author.

E ven after the end of the Cold War, cold currents persist in the Korean peninsula on the heavily armed and forti-fied Military Demarcation Line (MDL) and De-Militarized Zone (DMZ). Almost two million soldiers are packed in a land about the size of the State of Utah.

The US often cites North Korea as a major security threat to it. If the North Korean missile that crossed over Japan but never near US territory constitutes a threat, then the US has to admit that North Koreans will feel a genuine and immediate threat from American troops who often carry out large-scale war exercises against them. Since the South has conspicuously built up its military with ultramodern arms, the urgency of the US mission to defend or deter against possible North Korean aggression seems to have faded. The US force in South Korea is no longer considered to be the guarantor of peace, but it seems to be the cause of the fragility of peace, and of tension.

North Korea's Predicament

Contrary to conventional belief, North Korea is not consid-ered to be in a position to wage a war against South Korea or the US; to do so would be suicide. If North Korea is driven into a corner by outside forces, however, it possesses the ca-pacity to inflict huge casualties to the South before it suc-cumbs. Its artillery can pour down on Seoul where a quarter of the population resides, and its short- and medium-range missiles can strike a dozen nuclear reactors, turning the en-tire South Korea into an inferno.

General Gary Luck, former commander of the US forces in South Korea and US–South Korea Combined Forces Command (CFC), estimated that a million people, including as many as 100,000 Americans, would have been killed when the US nearly plunged into a conflict in mid-1994 over the Nuclear Non-Proliferation Treaty (NPT) crisis with the North. The eventual outcome could be the extinction of the North Korean regime, but could the US justify such an armed conflict? South Koreans may be the first to oppose such US actions against their brethren in the North as they did during the NPT crisis.

Contrary to once favored predictions, North Korea did

not collapse, and it shows no signs of implosion either in spite of its dragging economic blights. And many now believe it should not collapse, since collapse may mean the next Korean War. So the military stalemate continues.

Although North Korea is in the mire of economic crisis, its main aim seems not to be economic aid but political gain. It perceives the US forces in the South to be the most serious security threat. North Korea wants to remove the threat; otherwise it seems that it has to continue its missile and weapons of mass destruction programs at the sacrifice of its people's welfare. In view of its grave inferiority in military strength, missiles are vitally important to North Korea for survival of the regime. Therefore, . . . economic incentives alone . . . are not likely to get North Korea to give up its one remaining bargaining chip, the missile program.

North Korea's other bargaining chip, the suspected nuclear weapons program, has already been taken away by the [1994] Geneva Agreed Framework [in which North Korea agreed to halt its nuclear weapons program in exchange for aid in constructing civilian nuclear power reactors], even though it has not gotten what it was promised from the US. Thus, it seems North Korea does not want to take the risk of giving up its last leverage and end up not receiving the reciprocal measures. For the North it could be a matter of survival or extinction.

Between the US and North Korea, which would be able to take risks without jeopardizing their national security? The US, as the one and only super-power of the world today, would be able to afford to take such risks with a much greater margin of safety than the North. Thus, it is conceivable that North Korea wants the US to tie the missile deal to a peace agreement and the dissolution of the United Nations Command (UNC). The US needs to make a bold political decision to resolve this military stalemate of 50 years involving half a dozen countries in Northeast Asia.

Awakening Koreans Under New Leadership

Unlike his predecessors, [South Korean president] Kim Dae Jung urged the US and Japan to help the economically devastated North Korea. He also requested that the US lift economic sanctions on North Korea and urged the US and other Western countries to normalize relations with the North. He is trying to help North Korea be a member of the international community. His policy of reconciliation and cooperation, and the corresponding response from Kim Jong Il of the North, have led to multifaceted exchanges in humanitarian, social, cultural and industrial fields in ever increasing quantity and quality.

With further practice of democracy in South Korea, open discussion on real Korean problems from an objective and historical context is spreading steadily. South Koreans, with their changing awareness of their history and nation, may finally realize who North Koreans really are to them. Withdrawal of the US forces has also been advocated by increasing numbers of South Korean civic groups. It is conceivable that such advocacy may rapidly increase.

Dealing with Reality

Dealing with the reality of the North as it exists and waiting for North Korea to change gradually could now be the only way to advance. There is an urgent need, in the meantime, for the lifting of sanctions on the DPRK by the US, and then the DPRK would be able to earn more foreign exchange and buy more oil, rice and medicines. And its children would not suffer from malnutrition. The Americans have the overwhelming military and economic strength. If it would move forward with wisdom and generosity then the way would be open for the economic and political transformation of North Korea, and a peace treaty between the two Koreas could eventually be signed.

Sharif M. Shuja, *Contemporary Review*, December 2000.

All of these changes in circumstances around the Korean peninsula produced an agreement for a first ever summit meeting in June 2000 between the South and North since its division in 1945. They initiated this one without intervention by a third party. Korean people are excited about the outcome of the meeting, where all their differences, mistrust, animosities and whatever else will be talked about and where they will try to settle the scores.

Judging from the number of dealings with the US that

have transpired during the 1990s, it becomes evident that North Korea has been eager to improve relations with the US. Notably, in recent years it has been conceding in many of its deals with the US: the complete freeze of nuclear activity, permission to inspect the underground facility and moratorium on missile tests in exchange for the same old US carrots.

Meanwhile, enormously increased exchanges and inter-governmental dialogue are progressing rapidly between the South and North, both of which are preconditions to normalization with the US. Unprecedented opportunities for rapprochement between the two Koreas and the US, as well as among other involved countries, are developing. It certainly looks like it is high time for the US to look to its long-term interest and begin the process of creating a sustainable peace regime in the Korean peninsula.

Time to Commit to a Peace Regime

The US has been insisting that North Korea must initiate tension reduction measures first. The US seems reluctant to be directly involved in a peace agreement with the North and wants to limit any agreement to being between the North and South. Should that be the case, the US would be better off by making South Korea a fully-fledged autonomous state. Among other things, it would return operational control of the South Korean military to the president of South Korea so that the South could guarantee any military pact it signs. By doing so, the US would be in a position to stymie any North Korean attempt to preclude the South from peace negotiations.

Once South Korea becomes a full-fledged sovereign state, a peace agreement can be signed between the North and South. Then China and the US can endorse the agreement as direct participants of the Korean War.

However, if the US does not relinquish its reins over the South Korean military, the US should sign with the North, while the North and the South sign a separate peace agreement simultaneously for completeness.

In any event it would be illogical and impractical, though, for the US to be completely away from any peace agreement, in view of its major role during and after the Korean War, and for maintaining stability in Northeast Asia.

Both Koreas should work out an arms reduction plan through their joint military commissions in accordance with the Basic Agreement of 1991 [Agreement on Reconciliation, Nonaggression and Exchanges and Cooperation]. Concurrently, the dissolution of the UNC would begin, and the US could pronounce that it agrees with the principle of eventual withdrawal of American troops as part of a comprehensively negotiated peace regime including repeal of North Korea's missile program.

Phased withdrawal of the US forces can be tied to the progress of the arms reduction and the dissolution of North Korea's weapons of mass destruction, including the nuclear and missile development programs. Sustainable peace in Northeast Asia can be achieved through the initiative of the US. In order to avoid future conflict among the neighboring countries, it would be desirable to make the unified Korea a nuclear-free, neutral nation with no foreign forces stationed.

It is the Clinton administration that changed its policy toward North Korea from the containment policy to the engagement policy, and that has brought us to the stage where the last remaining Cold War anachronisms can be swept away. Through concerted efforts by the directly involved countries, an unprecedented opportunity has come along for the US to initiate leadership to achieve a non-proliferation regime for stability and sustainable peace in Northeast Asia by ending the so-called Forgotten Korean War and bringing American soldiers home after 50 years.

> "*A peace treaty negotiated solely between the United States and North Korea would be a travesty of history.*"

The United States Should Not Make Peace with North Korea

Larry M. Wortzel

In the following viewpoint, Larry M. Wortzel argues that the United States should not go out of its way to negotiate a peace treaty with North Korea. Such an agreement would give a diplomatic victory to the North Korean regime that it does not deserve, and would slight the contributions made by other nations that participated in the Korean War. He contends that the Korean War was a prime example of United Nations military intervention and that the only proper way to formally end the Korean War would be a negotiated treaty between North Korea and the United Nations. Wortzel is director of Asian Studies Center at the Heritage Foundation, a conservative policy research organization. He received assistance for this essay from research assistant Paolo Pasicolan.

As you read, consider the following questions:
1. How many nations joined with the United States and South Korea to fight in Korea, according to Wortzel?
2. How did the United Nations become involved in Korea in 1950, according to the author?
3. Why is North Korea pressing for a bilateral peace treaty, according to Wortzel?

From "Why North Korea Should Sign a Peace Treaty with the U.N., Not the U.S.," by Larry M. Wortzel, *Heritage Foundation Executive Memorandum*, May 17, 2001. Copyright © 2001 by The Heritage Foundation. Reprinted with permission.

[The Korean War] was arguably the first major international conflict sanctioned by the United Nations in which foreign forces fought side-by-side under its banner. Although initially the willingness of U.N. member nations to commit their troops to the war was uncertain, 15 countries eventually joined forces with the United States and South Korea to fight for the United Nations Command in Korea.

The war in Korea lasted for only three years, but it claimed the lives of a million people before an armistice was negotiated in 1953, effectively ending the fighting. The agreement, however, fell short of establishing permanent peace. Officials at the U.S. Department of State are now considering signing a bilateral treaty with North Korea to formally end the war and establish direct relations. Though a noble goal, a peace treaty negotiated solely between the United States and North Korea would be a travesty of history. Moreover, it would hand Kim Jong-il, leader of the North and son of the man who first sent communist forces to invade the South, a major diplomatic success—a direct treaty with the United States, but one that ignores the significant contributions of the other U.N. countries that fought to defend South Korea.

The more appropriate policy for the Bush Administration would be to insist that any treaty designed to establish permanent peace on the Korean Peninsula be negotiated between the formal warring parties: the United Nations and North Korea.

The U.N. Forces in the Korean War

The Korean War began when the People's Army of North Korea crossed the 38th parallel to invade the South on June 25, 1950. The U.N. Security Council convened an emergency session and passed a resolution calling for the "immediate cessation of hostilities" on the Peninsula, as well as the withdrawal of the North's forces from the South. Russia, an ally of the North, was unable to veto the measure because it had withdrawn its representative six months earlier to boycott Taiwan's control of China's seat on the Security Council. Two days later, after the South appealed for greater assistance, the council passed a resolution recommending that

U.N. nations assist the South "to repel the armed attack and to restore international peace and security to the area." A multinational force was quickly formed under the unified command of the United States.

An Evil Regime

On June 25, 1950, a date that should live in infamy, North Korea started a war that killed millions of people, greatly aggravated East-West tensions and burdened U.S. relations with China and Russia with problems that remain to this day. . . .

As clearly as Adolf Hitler is to be blamed for starting World War II, North Korea's dictator Kim Il Sung must be blamed for attacking South Korea, coercing a reluctant [Soviet leader Joseph] Stalin to back his aggression, and thus implanting the Cold War all over Asia. But unlike Nazi Germany, now safely a thing of the past, Kim Il Sung's regime of cruelty and terror still rules North Korea and keeps denying every aspect of the holocaust it caused.

Amazingly, though, the victims of North Korea's policies— the United States, South Korea, Japan, China and Europe— have been donating more and more aid to this source of evil.

Fred C. Ikle, *Washington Post*, June 23, 2000.

This was the first time that the United Nations established a military force to intervene in an international conflict. Although the U.S. military dominated the coalition effort, thousands of other soldiers fought under the U.N. flag, including troops from Ethiopia, Colombia, and Luxembourg. A total of 150,000 foreign servicemen fought in Korea, with over 11,000 wounded and 5,000 either killed or listed as missing in action. The United Kingdom was the first to send troops to the front lines; by war's end, of the 60,000 British soldiers who had fought there, 4,436 had spilled blood on Korean soil. Canada had the fourth largest contingent; of its 27,000 soldiers, there were 1,556 casualties. Australia sent 17,164 soldiers and had 1,416 casualties. The Turkish forces numbered 15,000 and sustained 3,216 casualties. . . .

In most instances, the U.N. forces were grossly outnumbered by the invading Chinese forces, who had entered the war in late 1950. Yet they stayed their ground to buy time for the American-led counteroffensive.

Seeking Permanent Peace

The last two years of the Korean War deteriorated into a battle of attrition along the original border between the two sides prior to the invasion. Weary of bloodshed, U.S. Army General Mark W. Clark, Commander in Chief of the United Nations Command, and representatives from North Korea and China signed a Military Armistice Agreement on July 27, 1953—an armistice between North Korean forces and the United Nations, not the United States. The government of South Korea refused to sign the treaty, finding the prospect of a divided Korea unacceptable.

At the insistence of Pyongyang, the U.S. Department of State is currently negotiating an exclusive peace treaty between the United States and North Korea that would replace the existing armistice. Although peace on the Peninsula is long overdue, this is the wrong way to close the book on one of the epoch-defining events of the 20th century. A peace treaty solely between the United States and North Korea would cloud the legacy of those 37,895 soldiers who fought and died together under the U.N. flag. Although a bilateral treaty may be politically expedient, history should not be ignored for purposes of convenience.

A bilateral peace treaty between the United States and North Korea, moreover, would give an enormous diplomatic victory to a North Korean regime that has refused to end the war against the South. The reason Pyongyang wants to negotiate with the United States alone is that it hopes to secure monetary concessions in exchange for peace. Later, North Korea could argue for the withdrawal of U.S. forces. The memories of the war, however, are far too valuable to be used as a bargaining chip in political discussions between Pyongyang and Washington.

On this issue, there should be no compromise. The 1953 armistice ending the Korean War was signed by the U.N. commander; a peace treaty should be an extension of that agreement. Therefore, the Bush Administration should direct the State Department to cease its unilateral efforts and insist instead that North Korea sign a peace treaty with the United Nations to formally end the North's 50-year-old hostilities toward the South.

Periodical Bibliography

The following articles have been selected to supplement the diverse views presented in this chapter.

Doug Bandow	"South Korea Should Be Kicked Off the U.S. Defense Dole," *USA Today Magazine*, March 1999.
Bruce Cumings	"The Fluke That Wrecked East Asia Policy," *American Prospect*, March 15, 2001.
Nicholas Eberstadt	"Korean Security: The Millennial Moment," *Asian Wall Street Journal*, January 15, 2001.
Nicholas Eberstadt and Richard J. Ellings	"The Next Hot Spot," *Washington Times*, May 23, 2001.
John Feffer	"North Korea and the Politics of Engagement," *Peace Review*, September 1999.
David Ignatius	"The Korea Challenge," *Washington Post*, January 7, 2001.
Fred C. Ikle	"Evil Without End?" *Washington Post*, June 23, 2000.
Henry A. Kissinger	"A Road Through Seoul," *Washington Post*, March 6, 2001.
Hwal Woong Lee	"North Won't Deal While U.S. Troops Stay," *Los Angeles Times*, August 16, 1999.
Edward A. Olsen	"U.S. Security Policy and the Two Koreas," *World Affairs*, Spring 2000.
Christopher Lim Park	"Turbulent Relations: Redirecting U.S. Foreign Policy Toward North Korea," *Harvard International Review*, Summer 1998.
Sharif M. Shuja	"North Korea and the West," *Contemporary Review*, December 2000.
Leon V. Sigal	"Countdown on Korea," *American Prospect*, August 27, 2001.
Joel S. Witt	"North Korea: The Leader of the Pack," *Washington Quarterly*, Winter 2001.
Jon B. Wolfstahl	"North Korea: Hard Line Is Not the Best Line," *Los Angeles Times*, March 7, 2001.

CHAPTER 4

What Is the Future of North and South Korea?

Chapter Preface

A question that looms over all others when discussing the future of North and South Korea is whether their Cold War–imposed division will ever end and the two nations be reunited, much as East and West Germany were reunited in 1990. The governments of both North and South Korea have consistently proclaimed unification as a goal, but both have envisioned a united Korea on their terms and under their rule. Recent breakthroughs in Korean diplomacy have raised both hopes and doubts about Korean reunification.

North/South rapprochement got a boost with the 1997 election of Kim Dae Jung as president of South Korea. In 1998, he announced a "Sunshine Policy" of promoting dialogue with the North. His openness toward North Korea culminated in June 2000 with an unprecedented trip to North Korea and a summit visit with North Korean leader Kim Jong Il. A few months later, one hundred people from both nations crossed the border to visit family members separated from each other since the Korean War. North and South Korean athletes also marched together under one flag at the opening ceremonies of the 2000 Summer Olympics in Australia.

It is unclear whether these largely symbolic steps are a precursor to true reunification. South Koreans have criticized Kim Dae Jung's "Sunshine Policy" for promising rewards to a North Korean regime that has made few responses to South Korean proposals and taken few steps to open up its society. Opponents also argue that reunification would be costly, in large part because of the gross disparity between the two nations' economies—South Korea's per capita income in 2000 was $13,200, twelve times larger than North Korea's estimated $1,090. Studies based on Germany's 1990 reunification have estimated that the costs for Korea's reunification could run in the hundreds of billions of dollars. South Koreans debate whether such costs are worth it. "Despite the high price," write *Maclean's* magazine reporters Tom Fennell and Susan Oh following the historic June 2000 summit, "polls show that most of South Korea's 46 million people want to unite. 'It's not a matter of cost,' says Kim Hyun Ho, 'but of national pride.'" However, Doug Struck, a *Washington Post* reporter, believes that, for many South Koreans, reunification "is a goal recited with an understood wink. While virtually everyone in South Korea vows allegiance to it, few people actually want it to happen very soon, if at all." The viewpoints in this chapter examine reunification and other key questions concerning the future of the two Koreas.

"It is time . . . to think about how to make Korean reunification a success—because success or no, reunification is coming."

Korean Reunification May Be Imminent

Nicholas Eberstadt

Nicholas Eberstadt is a scholar at the American Enterprise Institute, a conservative research institution. He has published and edited several books on Korea, including *The End of North Korea* and *Korea's Future and the Great Powers*. In the following viewpoint, he argues that North Korea might collapse and be absorbed within South Korea faster than many people expect. South Korea and the relevant world powers—the United States, Japan, Russia, and China—must be prepared for such an eventuality. Governments of these countries can cooperate to help improve the chances for a rapid and peaceful reunification of the two Koreas.

As you read, consider the following questions:

1. What are some of the economic costs and benefits to South Korea of reunification, according to Eberstadt?
2. Why should Russia and China consider Korean reunification to be in their own interests, according to the author?
3. What can and should the United States do to promote reunification, in Eberstadt's view?

Whatever their differences, the five governments that must contend most directly with Pyongyang—Seoul, Washington, Beijing, Tokyo, and Moscow—all assume that a rapid reunification of Korea is not only unlikely, but would run contrary to their national interests if it occurred. In fact, a rapid implosion of the North is more likely than a gradual reunification, and with the opposite range of consequences.

The cherished vision of a gradual and orderly drawing together of the two Koreas is today nothing more than a fantasy. As time goes on, North Korea will only grow poorer and more dangerous. For all parties affected, the faster reunification takes place, the better. Many details of reunification remain uncertain, but Western powers must begin to consider what a sudden reintegration might mean. The Korean question is no longer a problem that can be postponed and then muddled through.

A Widening Gulf

The vision of a gradual reintegration of the two Korean economies that many South Koreans so fondly entertain assumes that North Korea's government will someday embrace a program of economic liberalization and somehow survive to complete the decades of transformation the program would entail. Yet Pyongyang to date has vigorously opposed any liberalization of economic policies worthy of the name. There is nothing to suggest that North Korea is contemplating any such reorientation. The weight of the evidence, furthermore, indicates that the leadership believes economic liberalization would be lethal for the regime. If the North cleaves to its traditional policy, the most likely outlook is continued economic decline. For the South, on the other hand, the most reasonable prognosis for the decades ahead is steady and perhaps substantial economic growth. Under such circumstances, both the relative and the absolute gap between the North's and the South's per capita income will continue to widen. Meanwhile, the cost of unification—the investment needs of North Korea in relation to South Korean output—will likely grow steadily and perhaps swiftly every year reunification is delayed. The further apart the two economies get, the greater the cost of bringing the North to parity with the Republic of Korea (ROK).

If, however, the specter of German-style unification expenses is terrifying to some South Korean policymakers, they tremble before a chimera. Any number of careful studies have pointed out that the bulk of western German transfers to the new federal states since 1990 have been for social welfare payments, not investment. There is no reason for these particular expenses to be replicated elsewhere—especially not in the ROK, which for better or worse still lacks most of the adornments of a full-fledged welfare state. Moreover, Korean reunification will yield benefits as well as costs.

In the short run, reunification with a poorer partner could help relieve South Korea's incipient labor shortage, reduce pressures on wages and other production costs, and enhance Korea's international competitiveness. A fusion of the two Korean workforces could increase purchasing power and living standards for the great majority in both the North and the South. Over the long run, as northern Korea's infrastructure and industrial capacity are renovated, all of Korea could experience dynamic supply-side effects. The flip side of North Korea's current infrastructural obsolescence is the coming opportunity to replace decrepit plants with state-of-the-art equipment embodying the latest technology.

The Weapons Ledger

If the economic prospects of a more immediate and deliberate Korean unification are decidedly less menacing than so often depicted, what of its possible political and strategic ramifications? Unfortunately, as difficult or contentious issues are deferred, the costs of maintaining the unstable balance in the Korean peninsula stand only to rise. From a financial perspective, in addition to underwriting military deterrence in South Korea, Western governments now envision substantial outlays to Pyongyang for economic and humanitarian aid. The "Agreed Framework" Washington reached with Pyongyang in 1994 is but one of several mechanisms for such transfers. To the extent that the great Pacific powers think about Korean security in a two-state framework, they will be ineluctably drawn to subsidizing the Northern system as its internal crises mount.

On a separate ledger, given the North's constantly improving arsenal, the extended survival of the Democratic People's Republic of Korea (DPRK) will raise both the probability and the expected intensity of out-of-theater security threats facilitated by DPRK sales or transfers of arms to extremist governments or terrorist groups in other parts of the world. While none of the policy alternatives facing the North Korean leadership today can look terribly attractive, a strategy of continuing to augment the North's potential to

On the threshold of unification

Lurie's World. © 1993 by Cartoonews International Syndicate, N.Y.C., USA. Reprinted with permission.

inflict devastation on both neighboring and more distant countries may appear more promising—and indeed, more logical—than any other option. After all, what sort of consideration could Pyongyang expect from the world community if "the North Korean question" were merely a humanitarian problem? To extend the life of the state, by this reasoning, it is imperative to upgrade the threat posed by weapons of mass destruction. Indeed, as best can be told, this is exactly what North Korean policymakers are attempting to do. For while the effectiveness of a conventional army will eventually be compromised by the decay of the national economy, the killing force of these particular instruments is much better insulated against such adverse trends.

Although North Korea's program for developing nuclear weapons is widely thought to be suspended, the DPRK has reportedly established a nuclear warfare command and may have one or more atomic bombs in its possession. The nuclear option, in any case, is only one component of the DPRK's overall program. North Korea has extensive capabilities for manufacturing chemical weapons, including nerve gas; according to some reports, it may have the world's third-largest inventory of these compounds. And North Korea has been working feverishly for decades on long-range missiles.

Although such threats would likely prove most burdensome to the United States, the only one of the four Pacific powers with truly global interests and obligations, all of the others would be affected by the destabilization that weapons of mass destruction can cause in distant venues, such as the Middle East.

North Korea Is the Nuclear Problem

Every government in northeast Asia can help improve the chances for rapid reunification. But two constraints loom large. The first is that neither China nor Russia can be counted on to cooperate in multilateral deliberations about what follows the end of North Korea. The second is that the allies most likely to cooperate in those preparations—the South, Japan, and the United States—have already restricted their freedom of maneuver through the Agreed Framework.

For obvious historical reasons, Washington's security relationships with Beijing and Moscow are vastly different from its relationships with Seoul and Tokyo. For similar reasons, China and Russia can be expected to regard an American design for a new Korea with considerable suspicion. China in particular has reason to appreciate the Korean status quo. Given its close economic and political ties with both Korean governments, the Chinese state now enjoys a more favorable position in Korea than at any point in the past century and a half.

Weighing against the impediments to cooperation, though, is the compelling fact that the current order in Korea cannot last. It is in both China's and Russia's interests to help shape the order that will follow. Moreover, Chinese and Russian interests coincide with the joint interests of South Korea, Japan, and the United States in fundamental respects.

If Middle Eastern oil exports were disrupted tomorrow by a crisis involving North Korean–made weapons of mass destruction, for example, China would suffer directly. Conversely, both Russia and China would reap commercial and security benefits from a successful Korean reunification. Therefore, they have strong incentives for approaching reunification together with the United States and its allies. The task for U.S., Japanese, and South Korean diplomacy, then, is not to convince Russian and Chinese leaders to submit to a Western strategy for Korea, but rather to encourage them to think clearly and realistically about where their own interests lie.

The Agreed Framework poses a rather different set of problems. This complex document outlines an extended schedule of financial, material, and diplomatic benefits that Pyongyang may obtain from a U.S.-led international consortium if and when the North passes a variety of milestones, mainly concerning compliance with the nuclear Nonproliferation Treaty but also involving such things as détente with South Korea and arms control. As negotiators on both sides have pointed out, the document is not a formal agreement, but a road map. Some, however, have observed that the agreement's ambiguities expose the United States and its allies to the worst of two diplomatic worlds, possibly obliging Washington to behave as if it were bound by treaty while permitting Pyongyang to decide when and whether it will honor its corresponding obligations. The range of envisioned Western-DPRK engagements restricts the range and scope of Western reunification strategies.

If Western governments are not to be ensnared, they must honestly recognize the Agreed Framework for what it is. The document does not solve the North Korean nuclear problem, but simply permits both sides to settle the matter later on. The North Korean nuclear "problem," for its part, does not derive from the technical specifications of the North's Soviet-style reactors, but rather from the inherent character and intentions of the North Korean state. The North Korean regime is the North Korean nuclear problem, and unless its intentions change, which is unlikely, that problem will continue as long as the regime is in place. If Western governments believe they can influence the nature of that state, they should assess their progress—or lack thereof—carefully and unflinchingly. But to allow this document to compromise preparations for Korean unification would be a grave mistake.

Southern Hospitality

The Western countries with the greatest prospective influence on Korea's reunification are South Korea, the United States, and Japan. What sorts of things could each of them do, bilaterally or multilaterally, to improve the odds of a free, peaceful, and successful reunification? As a first but vital step, Seoul should make preparation an immediate national priority and begin to design long-range policies. Political leadership in the South must increase the South Korean public's awareness of the tests that lie ahead and make the case that these tests can only be successfully surmounted by sensible strategy and concerted collective effort.

If a free and peaceful reunification is indeed consummated, the subsequent success of the project will also depend greatly on the dynamism of the South's economy, the resilience of its society, and the stability of its polity. Despite the South's great strides in these areas over the past generation, there is unfinished business in each of them.

Preventing war and forging a successful reunification will

require close cooperation with all the South's allies, including Japan. Although Seoul's ties to Tokyo have been deepening and warming for decades, there is ample room for improvement here, as well.

With regard to North Korea, the South must begin to think not only about deterrence but [also] about reconciliation. Healing the wounds of divided Korea promises to be a monumental task—one that may take generations to complete. But the process can begin now. Committing the South to a "malice toward none" policy after Korean unification, and to guaranteeing ordinary northerners the same civil and political rights as southerners, would send an important and stabilizing message. Working to open lines of communication and expand people-to-people contacts could increase familiarity and reduce misunderstandings on both sides. South Korean society today is strong enough to withstand any attempts Pyongyang might make to manipulate such overtures; Seoul would be wise to capitalize on that strength.

The United States can shape the prospects for Korea's reunification through diverse instruments, but its unique and indispensable contribution is in the realm of security. Just as the U.S. military commitment to the South has been the sine qua non of deterrence on the peninsula, a vibrant U.S.–South Korean security relationship in a united Korea will be critical to the success of reunification.

For Washington, however, preparing for Korean reunification will mean more than thinking about bases and planes. As the world's predominant economy, and as the presumptive leader of any strategic Western initiative in northeast Asia or other regions of the globe, responsibilities for coordinating an international approach to Korean unification will almost naturally devolve on the United States. Managing such an effort wisely and effectively will be a tremendous task—no less taxing or delicate than the historic endeavor that united Germany in 1990.

Japan's Role

To consider Japan's prospective influence on Korean unification is to beg the question of Japan's role in the world. In this century, Japan has never had a "normal" foreign policy: before World War II, it was an insatiable and revisionist power; after its terrible defeat, it has been a meek, one-legged giant. To this day, it is difficult for the Japanese to discuss their national interests—even in the Korean peninsula, where those interests are so directly and dramatically affected.

For better or worse, until Japan can play a role on the international stage in the same manner as other industrial democracies, its contributions to a successful Korean reunification are most likely to be made through the two diplomatic channels that Tokyo is most comfortable with: international finance and multilateral institutions. Japan's government and the Japanese business community can begin now to focus on the potential of mutually beneficial economic cooperation in a united Korea and on the problems that must be avoided or solved if such cooperation is to bear fruit. In multinational forums, Japan could be a persuasive lobbyist for an effective nuclear nonproliferation regime. In the years ahead, Japan could use its growing influence at the World Bank and other multilateral development banks to encourage those institutions to devote their technical expertise and financial resources to meeting the challenges that Korea's reunification would entail.

The list of possible initiatives and policies could be extended and elaborated. The point, however, is short and simple. Northeast Asia can live with a united Korea—in fact, it could be considerably more comfortable with a single free Korea than with the present arrangement. It is time for statesmen in the Pacific and beyond to think about how to make Korean reunification a success—because success or no, reunification is coming.

| "No *major power in Northeast Asia sees its interests served by a unified Korea anytime soon.*"

Korean Reunification Is Not Imminent

William J. Taylor

William J. Taylor is an adjunct professor at the Georgetown University School of Foreign Service and an international scholar with the Center for Strategic and International Studies. A former army colonel, he has written numerous articles and books. In the following viewpoint, he argues that immediate reunification of North and South Korea is highly unlikely and probably ill advised. Many years of peaceful coexistence between the two Koreas and political changes—especially in North Korea—are necessary for reunification to realistically occur. The United States and other powers with interests in Korea should not push for reunification, Taylor concludes, but should instead pursue constructive engagement with North Korea.

As you read, consider the following questions:
1. What three fundamental realities must be addressed in any discussion of Korean reunification, according to Taylor?
2. How would reunification affect North and South Korea and the other major actors in the region, according to the author?
3. What American foreign policy actions does Taylor recommend?

Few subjects in the broad realm of international politics have received more attention in the post–Cold War period than Korean reunification (or unification, as most Koreans prefer). Existing studies touch many dimensions: geopolitical, political, military, economic, sociological, psychological, religious, philosophical, comparative; many are scenario driven.

The studies have been done by international organizations, government agencies, research institutes, and peace organizations. Why all these costly efforts? Mainly because of the international security challenges posed by the standoff at the DMZ (Demilitarized Zone) but also because of humanitarian concerns and international investment interests in Northeast Asia.

Three Fundamentals

Straight talk about the subject demands discussion of at least three fundamentals. First, Korean reunification may be sui generis [unique]. Many studies have examined the cases of other divided countries—e.g., Germany, Yemen, and Ireland—to identify what policies and processes work or fail to bring about reconciliation and reunification. Prominent among these have been studies of Germany.

There may be some worthwhile comparisons of the German and Korean cases, but they are few. Hans Giessmann makes a very persuasive case in the summer 1999 issue of *Korea and World Affairs*. His article, entitled "Korea and the Myth of 'Cloning the German Unification Model,'" illustrates that the many years of East-West détente in Europe, which gave East German leaders hope that they could trade on openings to the West for increased legitimacy of power, have no prolonged comparison under the juche system of North Korea (DPRK).

Rather, former President Kim Il Sung and his son and successor, Kim Jong Il, have chosen to promote regime legitimacy and survival through a policy of isolation. Of course, that could be changing, but, if so, many years of détente and political/social change will be needed before peaceful reunification can occur.

South Korea's President Kim Dae Jung stated in March

2000 at the Free University in Berlin that achieving Korean unification would be very difficult. He noted that the two Germanys had never fought a war and that their unification was preceded by years of cooperative exchanges. He concluded that "it seems out of the question that we should hasten territorial unification."

The Dangerous Status Quo

A second fundamental on the Korean peninsula is that, although North Korea would quickly lose a conventional air-ground-sea war against the U.S.–South Korean Combined Forces Command, such a war would quickly escalate with the DPRK use of weapons of mass destruction (WMD). The North's well-documented, vast arsenal of around 5,000 tons of chemical and at least 10 kinds of biological weapons (plus, perhaps, a few nuclear devices) would be delivered against South Korea (ROK) by long-range artillery, multiple rocket launchers, and short-to-mid-range tactical missiles.

WMD would be delivered against Japan by much longer-range Nodong and Taepodong missiles. The stark fact of life is that there is no effective missile defense against North Korean weapons in either South Korea or Japan. Hundreds of thousands among our allies would die, and there are 83,000 U.S. military personnel, businesspeople, and dependents in South Korea and over 100,000 in Japan.

What about future DPRK threats to U.S.-ROK/Japanese security interests? As we know, almost two years ago, the DPRK fired a Taepodong-1 missile across Japan. The highly respected U.S. Rumsfeld Commission report of June 1998 had concluded that a test of a Taepodong-2 missile could produce the capability to hit Hawaii and Alaska and, in about two more years, all 50 continental states.

There is no theater missile defense (TMD) in Asia, nor a national missile defense (NMD) of the United States. Most experts conclude that, even with a pending decision by the Clinton administration to launch a TMD or NMD of our homeland, we could not have such a system in place for another six to seven years. Thus, we are in a period of maximum danger in relation to North Korea even if Washington decides to deploy missile defenses. Moreover, some prominent Americans doubt whether the technology can be acquired for effective missile defenses. Certainly, Pyongyang is aware of all this and understands the political leverage inherent in the situation.

A third fundamental is that, while reunification is a great and deeply held ideal, especially for Korean families who have been separated for 50 years, it is not a short-term policy objective for any of the major actors in Northeast Asia. Why?

The Nations Affected by Reunification

North Korea. The No. 1 priority of the DPRK leadership is to preserve itself in power. The regime understands that near-term North-South unification could come only through a war it would lose, or by anarchy, coup d'état, or revolution among its starving and repressed millions. For the foreseeable future, Pyongyang wants controlled foreign assistance over the long haul to get through its times of trouble.

South Korea. Despite the near-miraculous recovery, given its recent economic malaise, Seoul cannot afford the staggering costs of near-term reunification, which have been estimated to be several hundred billion dollars. Nor is Seoul prepared for massive North Korean refugee flows to the south, which would occur under most near-term unification scenarios.

Japan. North and South Koreans share one thing: memories of the brutal Japanese colonial rule of Korea (1910–1945). Tokyo knows this and is reluctant to see a unified Korea capable of posing a serious security challenge to Japan. Furthermore, unification could lead to the withdrawal of U.S. troops from the Korean peninsula and, ultimately, the Japanese archipelago, creating a security vacuum in East Asia and necessitating very large increases in Japanese defense spending.

United States. Major U.S. interests in Northeast Asia are served by the peace and stability maintained in large part by the presence of about 100,000 American troops deployed in the Asia-Pacific region. Already under some pressure to reduce forces in Japan, the United States might find that its troops will not be welcome in a unified Korea, undermining America's security role and influence over lucrative Asia-Pacific markets.

And, with reunification, South Korea might be lost as the sixth-largest importer of U.S. arms.

China. In Beijing's view, the DPRK serves as a convenient, strategic buffer between China and the United States and Japan. Additionally, reunification would redirect large-scale South Korean investment away from China and into the reconstruction of the North. The collapse of the DPRK could trigger a massive flow of malnourished North Korean refugees into China, which is already burdened by overpopulation and growing unemployment.

Korean Ambivalence on Unification

[A] tenet of unification—that it is inevitable because division is aberrant—has a ritualistic quality about it that obscures the real ambivalence with which many Koreans themselves regard unification. It has always been the holy grail, but enthusiasm for it has fluctuated wildly over the past decade. . . .

The new ambivalence toward unification is manifest in several ways. Popular attitudes have changed markedly, and pragmatic considerations have intruded on what was formerly a normative discourse on unification. In part this is linked to generational change as those who remember a unified Korea (albeit as part of the Japanese empire) die off. It is also linked to the North's famine-like conditions, which only magnify further the anticipated costs of union. The result is that unification is no longer an article of faith, and the discourse has shifted instead to the added tax burden it would engender and the pressures it would place on an already weak social safety net. Hence, while it is still part of one's Korean identity to yearn for unification, a cautious "NIMT" (not in my time) consensus has emerged.

Victor D. Cha, *Orbis*, Fall 2000.

Russia. In relation to its Far East regions, Moscow shares many of the same concerns as China. The governor of Vladivostok is already concerned about a changing ethnic composition that could erode economic and cultural ties between Moscow and the Russian Far East. Thus, it was not surprising that Russia, in violation of a major human rights convention, apprehended and turned over to China the group of seven North Koreans who attempted to cross the border between Russia and China last December.

Thus, beyond rhetoric on the ideal of reunification, no major power in Northeast Asia sees its interests served by a unified Korea anytime soon.

To summarize the three fundamentals above: (1) comparative reunification models do not tell us much; (2) 50 years after the Korean War, we have a very dangerous military situation on the Korean peninsula; and (3) no major actor in Northeast Asia wants near-term reunification. So, where do we go from here? We should stay on the present course set two years ago by President Kim Dae Jung's "Sunshine Policy," now endorsed and expanded by the Perry Initiatives. For the foreseeable future, that course is basically set toward the objective of peaceful coexistence. [Editor's note: The "Perry Initiatives" refers to recommendations made by former secretary of defense William Perry in 1999. Appointed by President Bill Clinton to review U.S. policy, Perry proposed that the United States ease trade sanctions and begin the process of normalizing diplomatic relations with North Korea if that country agreed to cease its missile and nuclear weapons programs.]

A Policy of Engagement

The South Korea–induced engagement policy has involved Pyongyang in a series of dialogues with Washington and Seoul and, now, Tokyo. More important, the first steps of engaging North Korea over the past one and a half years have enabled the United States and its Asian allies to delay the systematic deterioration of the country through humanitarian aid and economic assistance. Shipments of aid and multimillion-dollar investments have not yet been met with reciprocity by Pyongyang, however, a sobering reminder that limited aid alone will not suffice to modify North Korean behavior.

Under the Perry Initiatives, the ball is in North Korea's court. Unfortunately, while the United States and its Asian allies wait for a favorable DPRK response, the leadership in Pyongyang insists that there is too much to lose and too little to gain by buying into the Perry package. Cognizant of this attitude, one might believe that the engagement policy will remain ineffective until the DPRK leadership changes its mind. This is a dilemma: The success of engagement is predicated on changes within the regime, but the communist leadership will stonewall for the sake of its own survival. So what can be done?

To break the impasse, the policy of engagement must take the next very big step to include mechanisms for building trust between the U.S.-ROK-Japan tripartite and North Korea. Without proactive measures to assure the North that its survival is guaranteed and its prosperity is in the region's best interest, Pyongyang likely will continue its familiar brinkmanship diplomacy. In short, if maintaining the status quo on the Korean peninsula is crucial for regional stability and getting through the period of maximum danger, all major actors in the region should do their part to ensure North Korea's place in the sun, as a recognized entity among nations.

How do we do this? First, continue humanitarian measures. Keep the international assistance flowing and keep pushing for verification of where oil, food, and medicine are distributed—though this remains a frustrating endeavor. Second, continue to affirm commitment to the Agreed Framework. Because this agreement remains the essential piece of North Korea policy, active implementation must be a high priority. KEDO's [Korean Peninsula Energy Development Organization] current financial troubles notwithstanding, irregular deliveries of heavy fuel oil and inconsistent flows of humanitarian aid to the North only incite the communist leadership to continue its brinkmanship tactics.

Swift execution of the Agreed Framework—(1) accelerated construction of the light-weight nuclear reactors, (2) lifting of U.S. economic sanctions, and (3) diplomatic normalization—does not mean making concessions. Rather, these steps are part of a strategic bargain. There is recent progress on this front. Third, move quickly on U.S.-DPRK normalization. Unilateral U.S. recognition of North Korea and the establishment of embassies in Pyongyang and Washington could be the next biggest stepping-stones toward earning North Korean trust.

Of course, there are many major issues to address, such as removing North Korea from the State Department list of terrorist states, signing a permanent North-South peace treaty, the status of U.S. troops on the Korean peninsula, and North Korea's nuclear and missile programs. Negotiating them after normalization would be far more effective than making them preconditions to the normalization process. U.S. recognition would open doors for regular high-level exchanges among key policymakers and military leaders to promote confidence-building measures. Improved ties would enable North Korea to gain access to economic assistance from international organizations such as the World Bank, the International Monetary Fund, and the Asia Development Bank.

Constructive engagement toward rapid peaceful coexistence with a long-range goal of Korean reunification? What do we have to lose? Yes, lots of money. What do we have to gain? Time to protect the security of the United States, South Korea, and Japan during this period of maximum danger while pursuing change in the juche system, which would work to the advantage of the oppressed North Korean people and permit progress toward the ideal of unification.

The alternative? Keep risking war by accident or miscalculation—where all lose. Constructive engagement is not just the best alternative; it is the only safe and sane alternative.

> *"The Sunshine Policy . . . is aimed at freeing both the South and North from the terror of war."*

South Korea Should Continue to Reach Out to North Korea

Kim Dae Jung

Kim Dae Jung, a longtime political dissident in South Korea, was elected president of that country in 1997 in his fourth attempt, winning a 40 percent plurality of the vote. He soon introduced what he called the "Sunshine Policy," a policy of open dialogue and reconciliation toward North Korea. His initiatives culminated in an unprecedented June 2000 summit meeting with North Korean leader Kim Jong Il in the North Korean capital of Pyongyang, and he was awarded the 2000 Nobel Peace Prize for his efforts. The following viewpoint is excerpted from a speech Kim Dae Jung gave to a gathering of peace activists on June 16, 2001, one year after the inter-Korean summit. He argues that his meeting with the North Korean leader was a significant event that advanced the causes of peace and cooperation between the two Koreas. He reiterates the fundamental principles of his Sunshine Policy and argues that North and South Korea should pursue peaceful coexistence, leaving reunification as a long-term future goal.

As you read, consider the following questions:

1. What are the underlying principles of the Sunshine Policy, according to Kim?
2. How many years might it take to achieve actual reunification of North and South Korea, according to Kim?

Excerpted from Kim Dae Jung's address to the Peace Forum on Jeju Island to mark the first anniversary of the Inter-Korean Summit, June 16, 2001.

The June 15, 2000 inter-Korean summit was a deeply significant event in Korean history as well as for world peace.

In particular, 2000 was the 50th anniversary of the outbreak of the Korean War, the greatest tragedy in modern Korean history. For 50 long years, the South and North continued the anachronistic Cold War without being able to shed the hostilities and conflict.

At this very point, Chairman Kim Jong-il of the North Korean National Defense Commission and I met and provided a dramatic opportunity for peace, reconciliation and cooperation on the Korean Peninsula. The entire world was surprised and delighted and cheered and supported us. It was a historic happening, indeed. It was a proud event that demonstrated the potential strength of the great Korean people. This has contributed not only to peace on the Peninsula but also in the world.

The Sunshine Policy

At my inauguration in February 1998, I declared to the Korean people and the world the Sunshine Policy based on three principles. First, we will not tolerate any armed provocation by North Korea. Second, we will not harm North Korea or try to achieve unification by absorbing it. And third, the South and North should try to coexist and interact peacefully through reconciliation and cooperation.

Despite various difficulties, the Government of the People has consistently maintained the Sunshine Policy. We urged all nations, including the United States, Japan and European Union (EU) members, to hold dialogue with North Korea and extend economic assistance. We took a clearly different attitude from that of successive past administrations.

Of course, we have not slackened our efforts to maintain the ROK-U.S. defense alliance and the cooperation among the Republic of Korea, the United States and Japan. But now, peace is our most important goal and object. The entire world supported our Sunshine Policy. I would like to take this opportunity to express my heartfelt gratitude to all peace-loving nations and their leaders, including the United States, Japan, China and Russia, for their support.

Summit Agreements

Chairman Kim Jong-il and I worked out the following four agreements reflected in the June 15 South-North Joint Declaration.

First was the understanding of the unification issues between the South and North for unification. Both of us accepted the fact that immediate and complete unification would be difficult. More than anything, we agreed that the South and North would coexist and interact peacefully. North Korea came very much closer to our unification formula of forming a confederation that calls for "one people, two systems and two independent governments," by changing its past insistence on "a Federation" to a "loose form of federation." Thus, the South and North were able to confirm the possibility of reaching agreement in unification policies at last.

Second was the North Korean agreement on the permanent stationing of U.S. forces on the Korean Peninsula. This could be the most important result of the June 15 inter-Korean summit.

During the summit, I told Chairman Kim, "The reason we insist on the continuing presence of U.S. forces is not merely for national security against the North. U.S. forces should remain on the Korean Peninsula after unification. That way, we can expect a power balance and peace on the peninsula where, uniquely in the world, the interests of the four powers—the United States, Japan, China, and Russia—converge as well as peace and stability in Northeast Asia. The reason that Western European countries demanded the continuing presence of U.S. forces after the collapse of the Soviet Union and East European countries was because it was a necessary and inevitable condition for peace and stability on the European continent." While I was saying this, I expected a strong counter argument.

However, he unexpectedly said, "I already know your thinking through South Korean newspapers. And I thought to myself 'how is it that President Kim's idea is the same as mine?' The continuing stationing of U.S. forces on the Korean Peninsula will be beneficial to our people."

When I listened to Chairman Kim's reply, I could not

help feeling that our ancestors were leading us on the path to lasting peace.

Third, we agreed on inter-Korean exchanges and cooperation. The South and North agreed to confirm the fate of members of separated families and prepare reunions and to cooperate economically. We have also agreed to undertake exchanges and cooperation in a wide variety of areas, including the social, cultural and sport fields. The South and North have a great opportunity to work for coprosperity and the restoration of homogeneity.

Fourth and last was the agreement for Chairman Kim Jong-il to pay a return visit to Seoul. This has great significance. Chairman Kim Jong-il's visit has to be realized if peace and cooperation between the South and North is to be firm. I believe that Chairman Kim's visit will be realized within this year as he has repeatedly pledged to faithfully implement the South-North Joint Declaration. . . .

Positive Developments

Positive changes have occurred since the June 15 inter-Korean summit. The three reunions involving some 3,600 members of separated families and the joint march by South and North Korean athletes into the opening ceremony of the Sydney Olympic Games moved not only the Korean people but all peoples in the world. Through Ministerial Talks and a Defense Ministers Meeting, the South and North pledged not to fight each other again. We have concluded four agreements to activate inter-Korean economic cooperation, including those on a guarantee of investments and avoidance of double taxation. We have also agreed to reconnect the Seoul-Shinuiju railway and construct an industrial complex in Kaesong.

However, as you know, there has recently been a temporary lull in the dialogue between Washington and Pyongyang and between Seoul and Pyongyang.

Despite that, we are not losing hope. I am firmly convinced that our Sunshine Policy will succeed in the end. When all things are considered, the Sunshine Policy is the best; there really is no other viable alternative. Moreover, it coincides with the interests and the yearning for peace of all nations, not only South and North Korea and the four big powers. The entire world as well as an overwhelming majority of our people supports the Sunshine Policy. More than anything, experts on Korean issues . . . are giving it unsparing support.

Progress Takes Time

Some find the results of the North-South peace process [since 1998] to be insufficient, and the pace too slow. In response, let me remind you that it took more than 70 years for the Soviet Union to collapse; and more than 20 years elapsed after Willy Brandt launched *Ostpolitik* before the Berlin Wall crumbled. And, I don't need to remind you that the United States' decision to establish full diplomatic relations with the Soviet Union in 1933 was not based on trust. Nor did the question of trust enter into the Nixon–Zhou Enlai Shanghai Communiqué in 1972, which began the process that led ultimately to the normalization of relations between the U.S. and communist China on January 1, 1979. As a matter of fact, all these relationships have commenced despite a lack of trust. North and South Korea, too, need such forbearance from the United States. We do not ask the U.S. to blindly trust North Korea; only that it continue its relationship in order to build up mutual trust. And ultimately, we ask that the U.S. understand the suffering of the Korean people after more than 50 years of division. The desire to reunite the nation stems from the Korean people's deepest soul-searching. Why must the Cold War persist on the Korean peninsula when it has ended everywhere else around the world? We need empathy for our efforts to resolve this last relic of the Cold War.

Sun-chul Yang, *Korea Society Quarterly*, Summer 2001.

Fortunately, some hopeful changes have begun to appear. When Prime Minister Goran Persson of Sweden visited North Korea in May 2001, Pyongyang made it clear that it would implement the June 15 South-North Joint Declaration and that it would carry out Chairman Kim Jong-il's promise to make a return visit to the South. At the same time, Pyongyang clarified that it would extend the moratorium on missile test-firing to 2003.

Meanwhile, on June 6, 2001, U.S. President [George W.] Bush announced the completion of the U.S. Government's

North Korea policy review and said his administration planned to resume dialogue with Pyongyang. This decision was made through, among other things, the Korea-U.S. summit in March and the ongoing close policy consultation between the two countries. I welcome President Bush's willingness to reopen dialogue with Pyongyang and earnestly hope that the planned U.S.–North Korea contacts will make meaningful progress.

It is also significant that the two Koreas agreed last week [in June 2001] that they would work together to open a new land route linking the South and the Kumgangsan mountains in the North as well as to designate the mountain as a special tourist zone. Just yesterday, the inter-Korean Ministerial Talks exchanged messages celebrating the first anniversary of the inter-Korean summit and pledging anew to implement the June 15 South-North Joint Declaration. . . .

Rapprochement between the South and North can be expected only when relations between the United States and North Korea improve; the Washington-Pyongyang and Seoul-Pyongyang relationships are closely interrelated. Success in one of the two channels does not guarantee peace on the Korean peninsula. The two routes of dialogue should be developed simultaneously.

My Administration will exert utmost efforts to enhance the ties between Seoul and Pyongyang and between Washington and Pyongyang at the same time. I earnestly desire to see the United States and North Korea engage in negotiations faithfully and responsibly and reap good results. This is the wish of all peoples of the world and this, of course, would promote the common interests of the South, the North and Washington. . . .

Peaceful Coexistence

In essence, the Sunshine Policy of my Administration is aimed at freeing both the South and North from the terror of war and realizing peaceful coexistence and peaceful exchanges.

Actual reunification is a future objective. The South and North should first pursue peaceful coexistence and cooperation with each other, and when they think the time is ripe, could be 10 years or 20 years, they can eventually be reunified.

Our Sunshine Policy is a truly difficult proposition. It requires courage and perseverance as well as faithfulness and wisdom. Our tasks will be many and varied. However, I firmly believe that the policy is the call of history. It represents the aspiration of all peoples and the Korean nation's only viable route to survival.

"All of this obliges us to view the current North Korea policy with mounting skepticism."

South Korea's Policy of Reaching Out to North Korea Must Be Reexamined

JoongAng Ilbo

South Korean president Kim Dae Jung's "Sunshine Policy" of seeking rapprochement with North Korea has been criticized by some South Koreans for giving the North Korean regime aid and support for too little in return. In the following viewpoint, taken from an editorial in the South Korean newspaper *JoongAng Ilbo*, the editors argue that North Korea has failed to respond to South Korean peace overtures and continues to demand reunification on its own terms. South Korea's policy of appeasing its northern neighbor must be rethought, they conclude.

As you read, consider the following questions:

1. What is the purpose of South Korea's peace policy toward North Korea, according to the editors of *JoongAng Ilbo*?
2. What examples of North Korean belligerence do the authors provide?
3. What must the South Korean government do, according to the authors?

The recent controversy over the "National Unification Festival" in Pyeongyang at a time when South-North dialogue has come to a deadlock may well indicate that this is a good time to wholly reexamine the North Korea policy that South Korea has been pursuing since the inter-Korean summit meeting of June 15, 2000. [Editor's note: On August 15, 2001, several hundred representatives of South Korean religious and civic groups were allowed to travel to North Korea to observe celebrations of Korea's anniversary of independence from Japan. Some of that group actively took part in ceremonies at a monument glorifying former North Korean leader Kim Il Sung, angering many in South Korea and possibly breaking South Korean security laws. The political scandal resulted in a parliamentary no-confidence vote against South Korea's Unification Minister and a reshuffling of President Kim Dae Jung's cabinet.]

Ineffective North Korea Policy

We believe that if the existing North Korea policy—an approach designed to convert North-South confrontation into a relationship of peace—has proven ineffective while fueling friction within the South, there is a need for the government to objectively reexamine the appropriateness of this policy and adopt necessary revisions.

Thus far, we have supported the administration's North Korea policy, believing that, to overcome national division and military tension, there should be efforts that promote engagement, exchanges and cooperation between the two sides for enhancing coexistence and reconciliation.

However, the South Korean government's appeasement-only posture in which Seoul has been endlessly pushed around by Pyeongyang's one-sided South Korea policy, amid an unchanging attitude of North Korea and steadily growing friction within the South resulting thereof—all of this obliges us to view the current North Korea policy with mounting skepticism.

The government said that at the June 15 summit meeting, North Korea had retracted its demand for the withdrawal of U.S. forces from Korea, did not insist on its unification formula based on a federation system, and renounced its call for repeal of the National Security Law [South Korea's broad 1948 law forbidding anti-government activities]. North Korea also promised to revise provisions of the Workers Party platform that called for fomenting revolution in the South.

Problems with the Sunshine Policy

The basic assumption of the government's Sunshine Policy is that North Korea's aggressive behavior, including development of weapons of mass destruction, all is the result of a sense of insecurity. The way to moderate this behavior, according to this line of thinking, is to remove the causes of the insecurity and reassure the North of its military, political and economic security.

One problem with this view is that it fails to recognize that regimes resort to aggressive behavior for reasons other than just insecurity. North Korea, for example, has been investing an enormous amount of resources for political needs and ambitions as well as for purposes of extortion.

The policy that has resulted from such faulty logic has flaws in its practical application as well. The first is that our goodwill gestures have been for the most part unconditional, lacking in reciprocity. We have been much too willing to provide assistance and other economic benefits without demanding in return that North Korea reduce military tensions, curtail its missile and other weapons programs and resume dialogue with the South.

Second, the Sunshine Policy has relied almost exclusively on "carrots" while spurning "sticks." We need a North Korea policy that balances rewards for good behavior with punishment for bad behavior, instead of relying solely on inducements.

Lee Hoi-Chung, address to the American Enterprise Institute and the Heritage Foundation, September 15, 1999.

The underlying rationale of the government's North Korea policy has been that since there is evidence of Pyeongyang's having changed recently, a helping hand should be extended to the North. Ever since the June 15 summit, however, scant evidence can be seen of any real change in North Korea.

During his [August 2001] visit to Moscow, National Defense Commission Chairman Kim Jong-il declared that the matter of U.S. troop withdrawal from South Korea is the most pressing issue. Meanwhile, Pyeongyang has not yet revised the Workers Party platform either, suggesting that North Korea's pledges have been little more than empty rhetoric.

North Korea has instead set out to sell its unification concept, a federation system. The recent Pyeongyang festival, too, might have well been part of these efforts.

Ambiguous Unification Formula

The top leaders of the South and the North said there are some points in common between the South's confederation system and the North's lower-stage federation, while agreeing to pursue unification along these lines. The government should have made clear its stance toward the two formulas, but it didn't.

There has been no specific explanation about what the particular points in common are and what differences exist between the concepts of confederation and lower-stage federation. The two formulas have not undergone any public debate, either. This has made the two approaches all the more confusing, leading to a situation in which no effective means of restraint can be seen even when the North's lower-stage federation idea is openly discussed in the South.

Riding the tide of this confusion, pro–North Korean elements have run roughshod over right-wing conservative forces, creating widespread divisiveness within the South.

In a National Security Council meeting, the government recently decided to take action against those who behaved improperly during the Pyeongyang festival after being questioned upon their return home. This is a case of putting the cart before the horse. A proper response would have been for the government official who had enabled this incident to occur in the first place to assume responsibility.

It is imperative that all aspects of the existing North Korea policy be carefully evaluated from an objective viewpoint. If the government continues to adhere to policy measures focused on the realization of Chairman Kim's reciprocal visit to Seoul, North Korea is likely to continue displaying a haughty attitude toward the South, further fanning internal friction in the South while sowing the seeds for further controversy and unexpected incidents. This is the time for the government to present a comprehensive explanation and propose measures on how it intends to proceed with its North Korea policy in the future.

"If North Korea went the Chinese way, South Korea would be spared the immense cost of an abrupt, German-style reunification."

North Korea May Attempt China-Style Economic and Political Reforms

Michael Parks and Gregory F. Treverton

Many observers debate whether North Korea will follow the path of China, its Communist neighbor and former closest ally. Since the late 1970s China's leaders have engaged in market-based economic reforms and a limited amount of political liberalization. In contrast, North Korea has remained a closely controlled economic and political dictatorship. In the following viewpoint, scholars Michael Parks and Gregory F. Treverton describe some of the changes China has made and suggest that North Korean leader Kim Jong Il may institute similar reforms. Such a development would probably delay reunification between North and South Korea, Parks and Treverton argue, but would make reunification less costly and problematic when it does happen.

As you read, consider the following questions:
1. What economic and political reforms did China undertake, according to Parks and Treverton?
2. What important differences exist between China and North Korea, according to the authors?
3. What steps must North Korea take to begin Chinese-style reforms, according to the authors?

From "North Korea Considers 'Going Chinese,'" by Michael Parks and Gregory F. Treverton, *Los Angeles Times*, January 26, 2001. Copyright © 2001 by RAND. Reprinted with permission.

Does the second visit in seven months by North Korea's leader, Kim Jong Il, to China suggest that the North is "going Chinese"? Is Kim contemplating something like the Chinese path to reform? South Korea's President Kim Dae Jung thinks so: "This shows that North Korea is deeply interested in the Chinese-style reform and open-door policy and that it is trying to become a second China." The Shanghai that Kim Jong Il saw last week [in January 2001] included a GM plant, a Japanese semiconductor factory and the stock market—none of which existed when he visited in 1983 and pronounced China guilty of "revisionism."

In the 1970s, China, too, was unable to feed itself and exported cheap consumer goods to buy grain. Its people lived by ration books—so much cotton cloth, so much cooking oil, so much meat—and by special allotments when a couple was married or a baby was born. It had come through periods of great starvation, earthquakes and floods and the political chaos of the Cultural Revolution and the Great Leap Forward.

Changes in China

At a crucial meeting of the Communist Party Central Committee in December 1978, "paramount leader" Deng Xiaoping introduced the first elements of a market economy, followed over the next several years by these developments:

- Letting farmers sell rice they grew themselves. This quickly led to the decollectivizing of agriculture and the fueling of the rural economy. As farmers earned money by feeding city folks, they bought consumer goods, and light industry began to boom. Heavy industry followed. The terms of trade between city and countryside began to draw into balance.
- Opening China to trade, foreign technology and, very soon after, foreign investment. China, too, had sought self-reliance—not as extremely as North Korea—but it was wary of the West, of Japan and of the Soviet Union. The goal was modernization, paid for with what were then just promises of future profits for those companies and countries that entered China first. One of Deng's first moves was to establish special economic

zones—Shenzhen on the Hong Kong border—where he pushed economic experiments, including a stock exchange and foreign management.

- Seeking better political relations with the West. China established diplomatic relations with the U.S. just after the Central Committee plenum ended. China began to deal methodically with old disputes with India, the Soviet Union, Japan and others, though it did "punish" Vietnam for its move into Cambodia. Overall, this was a different assertion of national pride.
- Relaxing the Maoist ideology. This would permit new political, social and cultural freedoms—a reward for the intelligentsia and an encouragement to people to take risks—required by the new economic approaches.

These changes were possible only with the consolidation of power by Deng in 1978, after the death of Mao Tse-tung in 1976, much as Korea's Kim Jong Il consolidated power after his father's death. They also depended on Deng's persuading party and military leaders that reform was still socialism but with Chinese characteristics. The party was still paramount, and the economic reform plan known as the "four modernizations" included the military.

A Possible Signal of Change

Kim Jong-il's late-January 2001 visit to China, especially to industrial plants and the stock exchange in Shanghai, is the clearest of several recent signals that the North is intent on embracing economic reform fuelled by heavy foreign investment. . . .

Kim said that he "highly approved of the changes that have taken place", changes that "show that the Chinese people's policy of reform and opening up is correct". The visit, Kim's comments and early-year promises of "great change" to come amount to a signal that North Korea is looking to embark on its own bold economic experiment.

Asia Monitor, March 2001.

North Korea is not China; it has fewer resources, a much smaller internal market and has never been self-sufficient in food. Its economic crisis is probably deeper than China's was in 1978, and its political sophistication and technical know-how is shallower. However, its situation is not much worse than that of the neighboring Chinese provinces of Manchuria in 1978. Its small size confers some advantages, and its political leadership appears more unified than China's was. And it has a willing partner in South Korea.

Going Chinese

The Chinese model seems adaptable for it, all the more so if it were accompanied by economic assistance from South Korea, Japan, the United States and perhaps China. Going Chinese would require several steps.

First, get party and military leaders on board, in part by showing them what China has done and still remained socialist. Kim didn't need to go to Shanghai to learn about China; it is no surprise that he took his senior military leaders with him.

Find the best economic drivers and gradually free them from government constraints. Work on agriculture and light industry. Slowly, carefully abandon central planning by letting market forces grow within the country and then be influenced by the global economy.

Allow North Korea to be exploited—at the right price—to get trade going, pay for modern equipment and technology and establish a new industry base. What North Korea has is reasonably skilled cheap labor. Its immediate future is not in high tech, but rather in shoes, textiles and other simple processing that is now leaving South Korea for cheaper manufacturing locales.

Create openings to those countries that can help—first of all, South Korea and the United States. The others would then be easy.

Liberalize the political system by pushing decision-making downward, letting ideas bubble upward, and sending people abroad in significant numbers, which is already beginning.

Reunification Postponed

If North Korea went the Chinese way, South Korea would be spared the immense cost of an abrupt, German-style reunification. Reunification would be postponed, and its cost reduced as North Korea grew. This might be styled as "one nation, two systems," playing off the Chinese idea of eventual reunification of China, Hong Kong, Macao and Taiwan. South Korea would also find it easier to gather help from other governments if the North were pulled toward the mainstream of political and economic life.

There have been accumulating signs that North Korea's leaders have come to understand that they must change course. Going Chinese, adapted to North Korea's circumstances, is not a bad road map.

"It is by no means certain that North Korea will become a 'second China' given the significant . . . differences between the two countries."

North Korea Will Not Attempt China-Style Reforms

Yeon Hacheong

In January 2001 North Korean leader Kim Jong Il traveled to China for the second time in seven months. He met with Chinese leaders and toured an industrial complex. North Korean press reports and some outside observers thought this visit might signal a move toward economic reforms similar to those China had undertaken following the death of its leader Mao Zedong in 1976. In the following viewpoint, which first appeared in the conservative South Korean newspaper *Chosun Ilbo*, Yeon Hacheong argues that it is highly unlikely that North Korea will follow China's path of politically controlled economic liberalization. North Korea lacks China's domestic resources, is hampered by foreign criticism of its human rights record, and has yet to develop any foundations for a market economy. Yeon, an economics professor specializing in North Korea, teaches at Myongji University in South Korea.

As you read, consider the following questions:
1. What differences does Yeon say exist between the Soviet and Chinese models of reform?
2. What four general reasons does the author provide to back up his assertion that North Korea is unlikely to become a "second China"?

Northern Korean press coverage of the January 2001 meeting between North Korean leader Kim Jong-il and Chinese President Jiang Zemin, and Kim's visit to an industrial complex in Shanghai, are noteworthy in that they strongly suggest that the North intends to maintain its political system while attempting to revive its national economy through a process of politically controlled economic reform. First, this coverage seems to be an expression of Pyeongyang's desire to publicize its efforts to improve international relations in order to cope with a rapidly changing political environment, including the inauguration of the [George W.] Bush administration in the United States. Second, the North seems to be laying the groundwork for undertaking reform and opening for the purpose of economic recovery.

In this context, the news reports coming out of Pyeongyang indicate that North Korea intends to model its own reform and opening efforts after those of China, including establishing special economic zones based on China's experience with special industrial complexes. In fact, North Korea is already calling on South Korean businesses to invest in an industrial complex exclusively for South Korean companies in the Gaeseong and Nampo regions as part of its Chinese-style economic reform. Indeed, Kim's visit to Shanghai produced a kind of "Shanghai shock" among the North Korean leadership, as reflected in Kim's comments that "Shanghai has become an entirely new city" and that "one can no longer find remnants of 'old Shanghai' as the city has modernized so much."

Cage Theory

There are typically two ways in which transition economies undergo reform: that taken by the former Soviet Union, in which Moscow liberalized its political, economic, and social systems simultaneously, and that followed by China, in which Beijing maintained tight control on political power while introducing market principles based on a "cage theory" of politically controlled economic liberalization. However, even though Pyeongyang may be seeking to adopt a Chinese model of economic opening, it is by no means certain that North Korea will become a "second China" given the significant internal and external differences between the two countries.

First, progress in talks with the Bush administration, which seems to be leaning toward demanding greater reciprocity in dealing with Pyeongyang on such key issues as removing North Korea from Washington's list of terrorism-supporting countries, lifting economic sanctions, and negotiating an end to the North's missile development and export programs, are crucial for the North to attract much-needed foreign investment.

A Garrison State

As long as North Korea remains a garrison state, and unless it abandons its military-led political system, it will be impossible for Pyeongyang to undertake genuine reform and opening. Reconciliation and cooperation between the two Koreas are also likely to be limited in substance. This assessment stems not simply from a prevailing notion that the military is inherently resistant to reform and dubious toward peace, but rather that as long as the military enjoys priority in the allocation of limited resources and predominant influence in the management of state affairs, the chances for meaningful steps toward peace on the peninsula and unification of the country will remain bleak. . . . In a garrison state, reinvigoration of the private economy is destined to be subordinate to that of defense industries, with history showing that no garrison state has willingly pursued the promotion of peace.

Chung Chong-Wook, *Korea Focus*, March/April 2001.

Second, with significant natural resources and a domestic market of some 1.2 billion people, China has achieved economic development through market principles by inducing investment from Hong Kong and overseas Chinese investors. The North Korean situation, however, is quite different. In light of South Korea's own political reality and economic difficulties, Seoul is not in a position to provide huge amounts of investment capital to the North, a fact that will hamper South Korean efforts to promote inter-Korean economic cooperation.

Third, the international community is increasingly concerned about the human rights situation in North Korea. Increased international pressure on North Korea is thus expected due to a series of high-profile incidents, including the withdrawal of Médecins sans Frontières (Doctors without Borders) from the North in 1998, the adoption of a resolution last year [2000] by 30 leading European intellectuals calling for improved human rights in North Korea, and the scathing indictment of the North's human rights situation earlier this year [2001] by Dr. Norbert Vollertsen of Komitee Cap Anamur (German Emergency Doctors).

Fourth, North Korea has so far neither introduced a private ownership system for production nor developed a framework for establishing a market economy. Rather, Pyeongyang still places more emphasis on ideological adherence than economic incentives. Unless North Korea moves toward economic liberalism, including acceptance of the principle of supply and demand and the concept of democratic pluralism, its efforts at reform and opening will likely be confined to state-controlled initiatives.

External Dependency

How, then, should the recent changes in North Korean foreign policy be interpreted? North Korea continues to proclaim adherence to its juche ideology of self-reliance and to its "own style" of socialism. At the same time, however, signs of change in its foreign policy can be seen in the fact that it is now increasingly influenced by external factors in determining state policy.

Certainly, North Korea seems intent on alleviating its chronic food shortage problems by inducing humanitarian aid from the international community, and its energy difficulties with the provision of heavy oil from the United States and a light-water nuclear reactor being built by an international consortium, in exchange for freezing its nuclear development program. North Korea is also seeking to build up its foreign exchange reserves by adjusting its industrial structure, promoting exports, and attracting foreign investment.

North Korea's economic and diplomatic strategy during the current transitional period will likely continue to focus on "building a strong state" by forming beneficial ties with advanced countries. It is thus expected, in view of the current geo-economic situation, that North Korea will pursue pragmatic reforms in which it accepts outside assistance from such neighboring countries as South Korea, China, and Japan, while adjusting to external changes by maintaining strict control over its socialist political system.

Periodical Bibliography

The following articles have been selected to supplement the diverse views presented in this chapter.

Brian J. Barna	"An Economic Roadmap to Korean Reunification: Pitfalls and Prospects," *Asian Survey*, March 1998.
Victor D. Cha	"The Continuity Behind the Change in Korea," *Orbis*, Fall 2000.
China & North Asia (Asia Monitor)	"China Visit and Economic Reform," March 2001.
Bruce Cumings	"Summitry in Pyongyang," *Nation*, July 10, 2000.
Hugh Deane	"Korea: Division, Reunification, and Foreign Policy," *Science & Society*, Summer 2001.
Tom Fennell and Susan Oh	"Two Kims Bridge Korea's Two Solitudes: A Historic North-South Summit Could Bring Together Long-Divided Families," *Maclean's*, June 26, 2000.
Aidan Foster-Carter	"Sunshine or Sunset?" *World Today*, March 1999.
Frank Gibney Jr.	"No Marriage Vows Yet," *Time*, August 17, 1998.
Jei Guk Jeon	"North Korean Leadership: Kim Jong Il's Balancing Act in the Ruling Circle," *Third World Quarterly*, October 2000.
Nicholas Long and Frank Ching	"Can North and South Be Reunited? Two Views of the Future," *World Press Review*, July 1997.
Marcus Noland et al.	"The Costs and Benefits of Korean Unification: Alternate Scenarios," *Asian Survey*, August 1998.
Young-Ho Park	"North Korea in Transition?" *Korea and World Affairs*, Spring 2001.
Andrew Scobell	"Time to Think Ahead on Korea," *The Officer*, March 2001.
Fei-Ling Wang	"Joining the Major Powers for the Status Quo: China's Views and Policy on Korean Reunification," *Pacific Affairs*, Summer 1999.

For Further Discussion

Chapter 1

1. Assessing North Korea's military threat requires judgments both on North Korea's military capabilities and its military intentions. Do the disagreements expressed in the viewpoints by the U.S. Department of Defense and John M. Swomley center primarily on North Korea's capabilities or its intentions? Explain.

2. Both Swomley and Leon V. Sigal assert that North Korea is used as a handy justification by advocates for missile defense and greater military spending. What alternatives to greater military spending do they propose? Are these proposed policies realistic, in your opinion? Why or why not?

3. All the writers in this chapter acknowledge that North Korea's economy is in dire straits, but they differ in assessing North Korea's ability to project military force. Does the fact that North Korea is a very poor nation make it a greater or lesser military threat, in your opinion? Support your answer with examples from the viewpoints.

Chapter 2

1. After reading the viewpoints by Larry Diamond and Doh Chull Shin and John Kie-chiang Oh, list what the authors consider to be the fundamental building blocks and characteristics of democracy. Do the authors disagree on what democracy is, or simply on whether South Korea has achieved democracy? Explain your answer.

2. The depictions of North Korea by Hugh Stephens and the International Human Rights League of Korea (IHRLK) are starkly different. Which do you believe is more convincing? Why?

3. The IHRLK argues that North Korean propagandists promote a personality cult worship of its leaders. Does the Stephens viewpoint provide evidence for or against that assertion? Explain your answer.

Chapter 3

1. Doug Bandow asserts that an outbreak of war between North and South Korea would be tragic for Koreans but would not affect the United States, suggesting that the United States should not interfere if a war begins. Do you agree or disagree with this assessment? Does Glenn Baek offer any specific U.S. interests in defending South Korea? Explain.

2. Glenn Baek describes growing local opposition to American soldiers in South Korea, but he goes on to defend America's presence. Do you believe that the United States should withdraw its troops if a majority of South Koreans demand it? Why or why not?

3. What are the main differences between Christopher Cox's and David Wright's evaluations of past U.S. efforts to engage with North Korea? Do Wright and Cox have different measures of what constitutes success? Explain.

4. Indong Oh urges that the United States restore sovereignty to South Korea. In what respects does he say South Korea is not at present a fully sovereign nation? Do you agree or disagree with this assertion? Why?

5. After reading the arguments of Indong Oh and Larry M. Wortzel, do you believe that peace between North and South Korea depends on initiatives from the United States, the United Nations, or the Koreas? Explain your answer.

Chapter 4

1. Nicholas Eberstadt's and William J. Taylor's articles were first written in 1997 and 1999, respectively. Has enough time passed to assess their arguments in hindsight, in your opinion? Which author's predictions concerning Korean reunification have been more accurate, in your view? Explain.

2. After reading the arguments and views by Eberstadt, Taylor, Kim Dae Jung, and the *JoongAng Ilbo*, do you believe that decisions on reunification should be made by the Koreans themselves, or should other countries such as the United States play a leading role? Defend your answer by citing the viewpoints.

3. Do Michael Parks and Gregory F. Treverton believe that economic reforms in North Korea are probable, or simply possible? What evidence do they cite that would indicate that North Korea's government is amenable to reform? After reading their arguments and those of Yeon Hacheong, are you optimistic or pessimistic that North Korea will change anytime soon? Explain your answer.

Chronology

2333 B.C.   According to Korean legend, the kingdom of Cho-
                   son is founded at the site of present-day Pyongyang.

A.D. 300s   Three kingdoms emerge on the Korean peninsula;
                   Buddhism and Confucianism are introduced from
                   China.

668   The kingdom of Shilla defeats the other kingdoms,
                   beginning a thirteen-hundred-year period in which
                   Korea is a unified nation.

935–1392   The Koryo dynasty rules Korea. Buddhism de-
                   clines in influence.

1200s   Mongolians invade Korea; they are expelled by the
                   mid–fourteenth century.

1392–1910   The Yi dynasty rules Korea. Confucianism replaces
                   Buddhism as the state's official ideology.

1592   Japan attacks Korea and is defeated.

1600s   Christian missionaries enter Korea; in response,
                   Korean rulers begin a policy of excluding all
                   foreigners.

1630s   Manchu armies from China invade Korea and
                   force it to pledge loyalty to China; members of the
                   Yi family continue as kings of Korea while paying
                   tribute to China.

1700s   Korea becomes known as the Hermit Kingdom,
                   maintaining little contact with any country outside
                   of China and Japan.

1876   Japan forces Korea to open some ports to trade.

1880s   Korea signs commercial treaties with Russia, the
                   United States, and some European nations.

1894–1905   Japan's military victories over China and Russia
                   give it greater influence in Korea.

1910–1945   Japan annexes Korea and rules it as a colony.

1945   Japan surrenders to the Allies. Following an Amer-
                   ican proposal, Japanese forces north of the 38th
                   parallel surrender to the Soviet Union; south of it,
                   they surrender to the Americans.

December 1945	Foreign ministers from the Allied powers meet in Moscow and propose a five-year trusteeship for Korea.
September 1947	The United Nations votes to sponsor general elections in Korea to determine its future government.
August 15, 1948	UN-sponsored elections are held in the South, resulting in the election of Syngman Rhee as president of the Republic of Korea (ROK); the Soviet Union and North Korea refuse to participate. The ROK's capital is Seoul.
September 9, 1948	Kim Il Sung, backed by the Soviet Union, establishes the Democratic People's Republic of Korea (DPRK) in the North, with Pyongyang as its capital. Both the DPRK and the ROK claim to be the only legitimate government for all of Korea.
1948–1950	Ongoing border clashes disturb the peace at the 38th parallel.
June 1949	The United States withdraws its occupying forces in South Korea, leaving behind five hundred military advisers.
October 1949	Mao Zedong completes his Communist revolution in China, leading to an American debate over "who lost China" and concerns over the spread of communism in Asia.
January 12, 1950	Secretary of State Dean Acheson states that South Korea is outside America's primary security sphere in Asia.
June 1950	North Korean troops invade South Korea. President Harry S. Truman orders U.S. air, naval, and ground forces to help defend South Korea. At America's urging, the United Nations passes a resolution demanding that the Communists retreat to the 38th parallel and later asks member nations to aid South Korea.
June–September 1950	North Korean forces occupy most of South Korea and pin down South Korean and American troops in Pusan.

September– October 1950	Allied troops under General Douglas MacArthur successfully land in Inchon, retake South Korea, including Seoul, and push into North Korea. They capture Pyongyang on October 19 and press on toward the Chinese border.
November 1950– January 1951	China intervenes in the war, sending hundreds of thousands of troops into North Korea. They retake Pyongyang and press south of the 38th parallel, recapturing Seoul.
March 14, 1951	Allied troops rally to retake Seoul.
July 1951– July 1953	Truce talks founder on the issue of prisoner repatriation. Fighting continues on a battle line just north of the 38th parallel.
1953–1956	North Korea collectivizes its farmland.
July 27, 1953	An armistice agreement stops the fighting. A 2.5-mile-wide buffer zone, called the dimilitarized zone (DMZ) is established along the final battle line just north of the 38th parallel.
1954	Negotiations in Geneva, Switzerland, fail to draw up a permanent peace treaty or settle the question of unifying Korea.
1956	After having the South Korean constitution amended to permit him to run again, Rhee wins a third term as South Korea's president.
1960	Rhee wins a fourth term as South Korea's president, but widespread student demonstrations lead him to resign. Yun Po Sun replaces him as president.
1961	A group of military officers led by General Park Chung Hee overthrows Yun Po Sun's government. North Korea signs military aid agreements with China and the Soviet Union.
1961–1979	Park Chung Hee leads South Korea in an era of "guided capitalism" in which the government concentrates on building industries and promoting exports.
1968	Thirty North Korean commando troops raid Seoul. Frequent clashes erupt around the DMZ.

North Korea seizes the U.S. intelligence ship *Pueblo* in the Sea of Japan.

1971   Kim Dae Jung almost defeats Park Chung Hee in a presidential election. North and South Korean representatives begin to hold talks about reunification.

1972   Park Chung Hee forces through a new constitution that gives him almost unlimited powers and provides for presidential elections to be decided by an electoral college whose members are chosen by Park supporters.

1974   Gunmen linked to North Korea attempt to assassinate Park Chung Hee.

1977   The United States announces plans for a gradual withdrawal of U.S. troops in South Korea. North Korea announces that Kim Il Sung's son, Kim Jong Il, will become leader upon his father's death or retirement.

1979   Political dissident Kim Young Sam is expelled from parliament. Park Chung Hee is assassinated by his own security chief.

1980   Chun Doo Hwan, a South Korean general, takes over the government and bans political meetings. Kim Young Sam is placed under house arrest. In May, political protests in Kwangju are put down by force; two hundred people are killed, according to official government estimates. Kim Dae Jung is accused of planning the Kwangju demonstrations and is sentenced to death.

1981   President Ronald Reagan announces that no more U.S. troops will be withdrawn from South Korea. He invites Chun Doo Hwan to visit him on the condition that Kim Dae Jung's life is spared.

1985   North Korea signs the Nuclear Non-Proliferation Treaty.

1986   U.S. intelligence detects evidence of a nuclear weapons program in North Korea.

1987   Responding to widespread demonstrations, Roh Tae Woo, a general and Chun Doo Hwan's anointed successor as president, declares in June that he will run for president in a free election based on popular vote.

1988 Roh takes 37 percent of the vote after Kim Young Sam and Kim Dae Jung split the opposition vote; Roh's Democratic Justice Party suffers defeat in parliamentary elections. South Korea hosts the Summer Olympics; North Korea refuses to participate. The United States begins a covert diplomatic dialogue with North Korea.

1988–1991 The end of the Cold War and the collapse of the Soviet Union deprive North Korea of its most important allies and economic partners.

1990 Roh joins political forces with Kim Young Sam. South Korea establishes diplomatic relations with the Soviet Union.

1991 Talks between representatives of North and South Korea lead to several agreements, including one not to use force on each other.

1992 Kim Young Sam wins the presidential election; he becomes the first South Korean president without a military background since 1960. South Korea establishes diplomatic relations with China.

1993 North Korea withdraws from the international Nuclear Non-Proliferation Treaty.

1994 Kim Il Sung, supreme leader of North Korea since 1948, dies; Kim Jong Il succeeds him. North Korea and the United States complete an "Agreed Framework" in which North Korea promises to freeze its nuclear program in exchange for assistance in building civilian nuclear reactors.

1995 Massive floods in North Korea exacerbate food shortages; the United States and other nations provide assistance; North Korea breaks with its *juche* philosophy of self-reliance in accepting aid; over the next four years, between 1 and 3 million North Koreans die of hunger, according to foreign estimates. Roh and Chun are arrested in South Korea on charges of corruption. They are sentenced to prison upon conviction in 1996.

1996	North Korea and the United States begin talks on missile proliferation. The United States imposes sanctions on North Korea for selling missile technology to Iran.
1997	A financial crisis in South Korea results in a bailout by the International Monetary Fund.
1998	President Kim Dae Jung of South Korea announces a "Sunshine Policy" of improving relations with North Korea through peace and cooperation. North Korea fires a medium-range ballistic missile over Japan. The United States, North and South Korea, and China begin rounds of four-way talks aimed at replacing the 1953 Armistice Agreement ending the Korean War with a permanent peace treaty; progress is hindered by disagreements over who should sign such a treaty and the presence of U.S. soldiers in South Korea.
September 1999	The United States says it will lift some economic sanctions against North Korea, which announces a halt in missile testing one week later.
June 2000	North Korean leader Kim Jong Il and South Korean president Kim Dae Jong meet at a historic summit in Pyongyang; the leaders sign a joint declaration stating that they have "agreed to resolve" the question of reunification. The United States relaxes some economic sanctions on North Korea.
August 2000	One hundred people each from North and South Korea travel to the other nation to meet with relatives separated from them since the Korean War. A second family reunion event is held in December 2000.
September 2000	North and South Korean defense ministry officials engage in official talks for the first time since the Korean War.
October 2000	U.S. secretary of state Madeleine Albright visits North Korea. She receives assurances that no plans exist to test missiles, but the two countries cannot reach an official agreement.

January 2001	Upon taking office, President George W. Bush suspends diplomatic talks with North Korea and orders a review of American policy.
June 2001	President Bush announces the completion of a North Korea policy review and calls for "serious discussions" on a "broad agenda" with North Korea. The North Korean government refuses to engage in talks, arguing that the United States is setting unacceptable preconditions.
December 2001	A report by the South Korean defense ministry concludes that North Korea possesses enough plutonium to construct one or two nuclear bombs but that it would take several years for North Korea to make such weapons.
January 2002	President Bush accuses North Korea of being part of an "axis of evil" for developing weapons of mass destruction.

Organizations and Websites

The editors have compiled the following list of organizations concerned with the issues debated in this book. The descriptions are derived from materials provided by the organizations. All have publications or information available for interested readers. The list was compiled on the date of publication of the present volume; the information provided here may change. Be aware that many organizations take several weeks or longer to respond to inquiries, so allow as much time as possible.

American Enterprise Institute (AEI)
1150 17th St. NW, Washington, DC 20036
(202) 862-5800 • fax: (202) 862-7177
website: www.aei.org

The American Enterprise Institute for Public Policy Research is a scholarly research institute that is dedicated to preserving limited government, private enterprise, and a strong foreign policy and national defense. It publishes books including *The End of North Korea*; its magazine, *American Enterprise*, often deals with developments in Korea and Asia.

Arms Control Association (ACA)
1726 M St. NW, Washington, DC 20036
(202) 463-8270 • fax: (202) 463-8273
e-mail: aca@armscontrol.org • website: www.armscontrol.org

The ACA is a national membership organization that works to educate the public and promote effective arms control policies. It publishes the magazine *Arms Control Today*. Documents and articles on nuclear weapons in North Korea can be found on its website.

Asia Pacific Center for Justice and Peace (APCJP)
110 Maryland Ave. NE, Suite 504, Washington, DC 20002
(202) 543-1094 • fax: (202) 546-5103
e-mail: apcjp@igc.org • website: www.apcjp.org

The Asia Pacific Center for Justice and Peace works with organizations in Asia in support of peace and social justice. It publishes the newsletter *Asia Pacific Advocate*. Its website includes an online e-mail discussion group on Korea.

The Brookings Institution
1775 Massachusetts Ave. NW, Washington, DC 20036
(202) 797-6000 • fax: (202) 797-6004
e-mail: brookinfo@brook.edu • website: www.brookings.org

The institution, founded in 1927, is a think tank that conducts research and education in foreign policy, economics, government, and the social sciences. Its Center for Northeast Asian Studies focuses on analysis and debate over issues concerning Korea and U.S. interests in the region. Its publications include the quarterly *Brookings Review*, periodic *Policy Briefs*, and books including *North Korea Through the Looking Glass*.

Center for Strategic and International Studies (CSIS)
1800 K St. NW, Suite 400, Washington, DC 20006
(202) 887-0200 • fax: (202) 775-3199
website: www.csis.org

The center works to provide world leaders with strategic insights and policy options on current and emerging global issues. It publishes books including *Korea 2010*, the *Washington Quarterly*, a journal on political, economic, and security issues, and other publications including reports that can be downloaded from its website.

Hoover Institution
Stanford University, Stanford, CA 94305-6010
(650) 723-1754 • fax: (650) 723-1687
website: www-hoover.stanford.edu

The Hoover Institution is a public policy research center devoted to advanced study of politics, economics, and political economy—both domestic and foreign—as well as international affairs. It publishes the quarterly *Hoover Digest*, which often includes articles on North Korea and South Korea, as well as a newsletter and special reports.

Korea Economic Institute of America (KEI)
1101 Vermont Ave. NW, Suite 401, Washington, DC 20005
(202) 371-0690 • fax: (202) 371-0690
e-mail: rbw@keia.org • website: www.keia.com

KEI is an educational organization funded by the South Korean government. It aims to educate Americans on South Korea's economic development and relations between the United States and South Korea. KEI publishes the monthly *Korea Insight*, books including *Korea Approaches the Millennium*, and numerous reports and monographs, many of which can be downloaded from the organization's website.

Korea Foundation

Seocho PO Box 227
Diplomatic Center Building, 1376-1, Seocho 2-dong, Seocho-gu,
Seoul 137-072, Korea
(82-2) 3463-5684 • fax: (82-2) 3463-6068
e-mail: publication@kf.or.kr • website: www.kf.or.kr/english

The foundation, founded by an act of South Korea's parliament in
1991, works to promote exchange activities between the Republic
of Korea and foreign nations. Its Publications and Reference Materials Team distributes books and other materials on Korea to foreign universities and libraries. Its publications include *Korea Focus*,
a bimonthly journal of articles on Korean society and politics anthologized from newspapers and magazines.

Korean Peninsula Energy Development Organization (KEDO)

Public and External Promotion and Support Division
600 Third Ave., 12th Floor, New York, NY 10016
(212) 455-0200 • fax: (212) 681-2647
website: www.kedo.org

KEDO is an international nonprofit organization established to
carry out key provisions of the Agreed Framework negotiated in
1994 between the United States and North Korea in which North
Korea promised to freeze its nuclear facilities development. The
organization works to help North Korea build civilian nuclear reactors and provide other energy sources to that nation. Its website
includes reports and press releases on its activities.

The People's Korea

2-4, Tsukodo-Hachiman-cho, Shinjukuku, Tokyo, Japan
03-3260-5881 • fax: 03-3268-8583
e-mail: pk@korea-np.co.jp • website: www.korea-np.co.jp/pk

The People's Korea, a bimonthly published in Tokyo, Japan, is generally viewed as an unofficial mouthpiece of the government of
North Korea. Its website provides archived articles from the paper
as well as speeches by North Korean officials and other information from North Korea.

U.S. Department of State, Bureau of East Asian and Pacific Affairs

2201 C St. NW, Washington, DC 20520
(202) 647-4000
e-mail: secretary@state.gov • website: www.state.gov/p/eap

The bureau deals with U.S. foreign policy and U.S. relations with the countries in the Asia-Pacific region, including North and South Korea. Its website offers country information as well as news briefings and press statements on U.S. foreign policy.

Websites

The Chosun Journal
www.chosunjournal.com

The Chosun Journal is a nonprofit website that seeks to inform the world about the human rights situation in North Korea. It includes articles, editorials, and testimonies from North Korean refugees.

Korean Central News Agency
www.kcna.co.jp

This website contains articles from the official news agency of the government of North Korea.

Korea.net
www.korea.net

Korea.net is a website produced by the Korean Overseas Information Service (KOIS), part of South Korea's Ministry of Culture and Information; it provides information on branches and departments of South Korea's government, articles on Korean culture, and a directory of other websites.

Koreascope
www.koreascope.org/english

Koreascope is a South Korean website that features news and links to South Korea's Ministry of Unification and a discussion hall where people can post their own views.

Korea WebWeekly
www.kimsoft.com/korea.htm

This independent nonpartisan website provides links to articles, book reviews, and other information on Korea.

Bibliography of Books

Tsuneo Akaha, ed.	*The Future of North Korea*. London, UK: Routledge, 2002.
David Albright and Kevin O'Neil, eds.	*Solving the North Korean Nuclear Puzzle*. Washington, DC: ISIS Press, 2000.
Charles Armstrong, ed.	*Korean Society: Change, Democratisation, and Social Movements*. London, UK: Routledge, 2002.
Thomas J. Belke	*Juche: A Christian Study of North Korea's State Religion*. Bartlesville, OK: Living Sacrifice Book Company, 1999.
Joseph S. Bermudez Jr.	*Shield of the Great Leader: The Armed Forces of North Korea*. St. Leonards, NSW, Australia: Allen & Unwin, 2001.
Michael Breen	*The Koreans: Who They Are, What They Want, Where Their Future Lies*. New York: St. Martin's Press, 1999.
Brian Bridges	*Korea After the Crash: The Politics of Economic Recovery*. London, UK: Routledge, 2001.
Adrian Buzo	*The Guerilla Dynasty: Politics and Leadership in North Korea*. Boulder, CO: Westview, 1999.
Adrian Buzo	*The Making of Modern Korea*. London, UK: Routledge, 2002.
Mark L. Clifford	*Troubled Tiger: Businessmen, Bureaucrats, and Generals in South Korea*. Armonk, NY: M.E. Sharpe, 1997.
Bruce Cumings	*Korea's Place in the Sun: A Modern History*. New York: W.W. Norton, 1997.
Larry Diamond and Doh Chull Shin, eds.	*Institutional Reform and Democratic Consolidation in Korea*. Stanford, CA: Hoover Institution Press, 2000.
Robert Dujarric, ed.	*Korean Reunification and After: U.S. Policy Toward a Unified Korea*. Indianapolis, IN: Hudson Institute, 2000.
Nicholas Eberstadt	*The End of North Korea*. Washington, DC: AEI Press, 1999.
Nicholas Eberstadt and Richard J. Ellings, eds.	*Korea's Future and the Great Powers*. Seattle: University of Washington Press, 2001.
Roy Richard Grinker	*Korea and Its Futures: Unification and the Unfinished War*. New York: St. Martin's Press, 1998.
Taik-Young Hamm	*Arming the Two Koreas: State, Capital, and Military Power*. London, UK: Routledge, 1999.

Selig S. Harrison — *Korean Endgame: A Strategy for Reunification and U.S. Disengagement*. Princeton, NJ: Princeton University Press, 2002.

Martin Hart-Landsberg — *Korea: Division, Reunification, and U.S. Foreign Policy*. New York: Monthly Review Press, 1999.

James Hoare and Susan Pares — *Conflict in Korea: An Encyclopedia*. Santa Barbara, CA: ABC-CLIO, 1999.

Helen-Louise Hunter — *Kim Il-song's North Korea*. Westport, CT: Praeger, 1999.

Seung-Ho Joo and Tae-Hwan Kwak, eds. — *Korea in the 21st Century*. Huntington, NY: Nova Science Publishers, 2001.

Soong Hoom Kil and Chung-in Moon, eds. — *Understanding Korean Politics*. Albany: State University of New York Press, 2001.

Ilpyong J. Kim, ed. — *Two Koreas in Transition: Implications for U.S. Policy*. Rockville, MD: In Depth Books, 1998.

Sunhyuk Kim — *Politics of Democratization in Korea: The Role of Civil Society*. Pittsburgh: University of Pittsburgh Press, 2001.

Donald Kirk — *Korean Crisis: Unraveling of the Miracle in the IMF Era*. New York: Palgrave, 2000.

Jongryn Mo and Chung-in Moon, eds. — *Democracy and the Korean Economy*. Stanford, CA: Hoover Institution Press, 1999.

Chung-in Moon and David I. Steinberg — *Kim Dae-jung Government and Sunshine Policy: Promises and Challenges*. Seoul, Korea: Yonsei University Press, 1999.

Robert J. Myers — *Korea in the Cross Currents: A Century of Struggle and the Crisis of Reunification*. New York: Palgrave, 2001.

Marcus Noland — *Avoiding the Apocalypse: The Future of the Two Koreas*. Washington, DC: Institute for International Economics, 2000.

Don Oberdorfer — *The Two Koreas: A Contemporary History*. Reading, MA: Addison-Wesley, 1997.

Kongdan Oh and Ralph C. Hassig — *North Korea Through the Looking Glass*. Washington, DC: Brookings Institution Press, 2000.

Jonathan Pollack and Chung Min Lee — *Preparing for Korean Reunification: Scenarios and Implications*. Santa Monica, CA: Rand, 1999.

Scott Snyder — *Negotiating on the Edge: North Korean Negotiating Behavior*. Washington, DC: United States Institute of Peace Press, 1999.

Dae-Sook Suh and Chae-Jin Lee, eds. — *North Korea After Kim Il Sung*. Boulder, CO: Lynne Rienner, 1998.

Roger Tennant

A History of Korea. New York: Kegan Paul International, 1996.

Michael V. Uschan

The Korean War. San Diego: Lucent Books, 2001.

Jean K. Williams

South Korea. San Diego: Lucent Books, 1999.

Young Back Choi
et al., eds.

Perspectives on Korean Unification and Economic Integration. Northampton, MA: Edward Elgar, 2001.

Index

Agency for Intelligence Service (South Korea), 62
Agency for National Security Planning, 62
Agreed Framework (1994), 98, 102, 108, 110, 115
  controversial in U.S., 99, 101
  duplicity of North Korea under, 111
  need for continued commitment to, 142
  North Korean perception of, 104
  nuclear weapons freeze and, 18
  problems posed by, 132–33
  reunification and, 129, 131
Agreement on Reconciliation, Nonagression and Exchanges and Cooperation (1991), 118
American Committee on Korea, 26
American Enterprise Institute, 127, 153
Amnesty International, 75, 80
Antiballistic Missile Treaty
  constraints of, 37
  U.S. and allies endangered by, 38
anti-U.S. sentiment in Korea, 20, 30, 96
  reasons for, 95
  tension caused by, 97
Apache helicopters, 29
Armistice Agreement (1953), 13, 18, 29, 89, 94
  between North Korea and United Nations, 122
Asia Development Bank, 143
Asia Monitor (newsletter), 157
Asia Times (newspaper), 41
Asian financial crisis, 48
asymmetric strategy, 23, 36
Atlantic Council, 105
Australia, 121, 125, 147

Baek, Glenn, 94
Bandow, Doug, 88, 89
biological weapons, 24, 37, 138
Brandt, Willy, 148
Britain, 69, 121
Bulletin of Atomic Scientists (magazine), 27–28
Bush, George W., 16, 18, 34, 148, 149
Bush administration, 120, 122, 161, 162

Canada, 121
CATO Institute, 89
Center for Defense Information, 28

Center for Strategic and International Studies (CSIS), 94
Central Intelligence Agency (CIA), 26, 27
Cha, Victor D., 140
Chang Myon government, 58
chemical weapons, 24, 36, 37, 138
  North Korean capability for manufacture of, 131
China, 95, 120, 145, 146, 164
  aid to North Korea and, 15
  attitude regarding U.S. missile defenses, 39, 41
  desire for unification with Hong Kong, Macao, and Taiwan, 159
  economic reforms in, 155, 156, 161–62
    possible model for North Korea, 158
  Kim Jong Il's visit to, 157, 160
  Korean reunification and, 127, 128, 131, 132, 140
  peace agreement should be endorsed by, 117
  role in Korean War, 13, 121, 122
  unlikely to support North Korea in war, 90
  U.S. normalization of relations with, 148
Chosun Ilbo (newspaper), 160
Chun Doo Hwan, 30, 45, 49
Chung Chong-Wook, 162
Clark, Mark W., 29, 122
Clinton, Bill, 18, 27, 108, 141
Clinton administration, 32, 110, 112, 138
  Agreed Framework violated by, 104
  aid given to North Korea by, 109
  change in policy toward North Korea initiated by, 118
CNN (Central News Network), 66
Cold War, 12, 87
  increased isolation of North Korea following, 15
  Korean situation a continuation of, 90, 114, 148
Colombia, 121
Combined Forces Command (CFC), 23, 114
Communist Party Central Committee meeting, 156, 157
Congress, U.S., 28, 105, 110, 112
  Committee on International Relations, 108
  hostility of, toward Agreed

Framework, 104
  Kim Dae Jung's address to, 101
Constitution (North Korea), 76, 77, 78
Contemporary Review, 103, 116
Cornwell, Rachel, 91
corruption, 15, 48, 61
Cox, Chris, 108
Cumings, Bruce, 27–28

defectors from North Korea, 78,
  82–83, 140
Defense Monitor, The, 28
Demilitarized Zone, 18, 32, 114, 137
  proximity of North Korean threat to,
  22, 23
democracy, 59
  development in South Korea, 15, 47,
  60–61, 116
    limits of, 55, 57–59, 63
      need for consolidation and,
      50–52
    relationship to economy, 48, 62
    significance of Kim Dae Jung's
    election and, 49
  spread of, after World War II, 56
Democratic People's Republic of
  Korea (DPRK). *See* North Korea
Deng Xiaoping, 156
Desert Storm military operation, 35
Diamond, Larry, 47, 80
*Disarming Strangers: Nuclear Diplomacy
  in North Korea* (Sigal), 39
Doh Chull Shin, 47
drug trafficking, 108, 109–10

Eagleburger, Lawrence, 35
Eberstadt, Nicholas, 127
economic sanctions against North
  Korea, 40, 66, 100
  need to lift, 42, 92, 116, 162
    for facilitation of negotiation, 105,
    106, 142
economy of Korea, 33, 49–50, 57–58,
  61–63
  American aid and, 108, 109
    need to reduce, 112
  in crisis in North, 21, 25, 100, 115
    need to continue humanitarian aid
    and, 141, 142, 163
  disparity between North and South,
  15, 90, 125, 128
  missile sales formerly a part of, 102
  need for reforms in, 162
    China could be model for, 155–59
      con, 160
    possibilities for cooperation and,
    106, 147
  reunification could improve, 129

see also economic sanctions against
  North Korea
Ethiopia, 121
European Union (EU), 145

Fennell, Tom, 125
Foal Eagle (military exercise), 32
foreign policy, 39, 40, 102
  of China, 157
  of North Korea, 16, 27–31, 152, 153,
  163–64
    changes in, 42, 116, 117
    isolationism in, 137
    socialist internationalism in, 69, 72
  of U.S. toward China, 148
  of U.S. toward North Korea
    change in, 149
    compared to policy toward China
    and Russia, 132
    engagement should be part of, 98,
    101, 106–107, 141–42
      to provide incentives for peace to
      North Korea, 103–105, 118,
      143
    imperialism of, 32, 69
    misguided campaign of, 27, 33
      armistice violated by, 29
      Pentagon involvement in, 28
      war exercises included in, 31–32
    need to rethink, 89, 100, 108, 109,
    112
    problems of containment and, 99
    reunited Korea should be a goal of,
    113
    Seoul should have voice in, 92
  see also Agreed Framework; economic
    sanctions against North Korea;
    Sunshine Policy
Freedom House, 75

Germany, 129, 134, 137–38, 148
  reunification in, 125
    expense of, 158
Ghauri missile, 109
Giessmann, Hans, 137
Greensburg, Pennsylvania, 35

handicapped people, 82
Harvard International Review, 30
Heritage Foundation, 119, 153
Hong Kong, 159, 162
Hoover Digest, 80
humanitarian aid, 141, 163
  necessity of continuing, 142
human rights, 45
  North Korean violations of, 46,
  77–78, 84
    against handicapped people, 82

international concern about, 160,
162–63
political prisoners and, 75–76, 81,
83
Russian violations of, 140
South Korean violations of, 53
hunger, 15, 83, 100, 140
cause of increasing number of
defectors, 78
sign of North Korea's failure to
provide for its people, 46, 79
Hussein, Saddam, 35

Ikle, Fred C., 121
Independence (U.S. aircraft carrier), 32
India, 157
Indong Oh, 113
Institute for Defense Analyses, 13
International Atomic Energy Agency
(AEA), 31
International Human Rights League of
Korea, 74
International Monetary Fund (IMF),
48, 49, 62, 143
international treaty banning
antipersonnel landmines, 27
Iran, 16, 99, 109
Iran-Iraq war, 102
Iraq, 16, 34, 35, 106
Israel, 35, 36

Japan, 31, 48, 156, 157
colonial domination of Korea, 58
end of, still celebrated, 152
democracy in, 56
involved in dialogues with North
Korea, 40–42, 141
involved in military exercises against
North Korea, 32
Korean desire for cooperation with,
145, 146, 158, 164
Korean unification and, 127, 128,
132, 134–35, 139
lack of missile defense system in, 138
vulnerability to North Korean
missiles, 23, 37, 138, 143
Jiang Zemin, 161
JoongAng Ilbo (newspaper), 151
Juche ideology, 70–71, 75, 76, 80
concept of human rights affected by,
67
Kim Il Sung the developer of, 64
Kim Jong Il's role in systematizing,
68
self-reliance stressed by, 15
June 2000 summit, 15–16, 92, 145–46,
152, 153
developments resulting from, 144,

147–49
hope represented by, 25, 40, 90
initiative for
exclusively Korean, 116
Kim Dae Jung's Sunshine Policy,
125
moratorium on missile firings
reaffirmed at, 23

KC-135 tankers, 32
Kie-chiang Oh, John, 55
Kim Dae Jung, 59, 62, 63, 96, 110, 144
challenge of consolidating
democracy, 53
changes brought about by, 50
election of, 48
political significance, 45, 49, 52, 60
because of longtime dissident
status, 47
future potential and, 54
June 2000 summit and, 15–16, 20,
40, 90, 92
1998 visit to U.S., 28, 101
presidential cabinet shuffle and, 152
request for economic assistance and,
115
with lifting of sanctions, 116
on reunification, 137–38, 146
see also Sunshine Policy
Kim Hyun Ho, 125
Kim Il Sung, 121, 137, 152
death of, 67, 92
as dictator of North Korea, 15, 74
foreign policy change and, 42
historic role of, 68, 69
ideology developed by, 70–71, 75, 76
personality cult inspired by, 77, 79
encouraged by Kim Jong Il, 80
with title of Great Leader, 45
Kim Jong Il, 15, 65, 72, 73, 77
China visit of, 155, 157, 160, 161
seen as signal of change in North
Korea, 156
Kim Dae Jung's attempts to reach
out to, 116, 144
meeting at June 2000 summit and,
40, 90, 92, 125, 145–47
personality cult encouraged by,
80–81
policy of isolation and, 137
reliance on military forces, 20
role in systematizing Juche ideology,
68
son and successor of Kim Il Sung,
45, 74, 79, 120
treatment of defectors from North
Korea and, 82–83
Kim Young Sam, 44, 53, 59, 92

Kissinger, Henry, 88
Komitee Cap Anamur (German Emergency Doctors), 163
Korea and World Affairs, 137
Korea Focus, 162
Korean Central Intelligence Agency, 62
Korean Central News Agency, 66
Korean Peninsula Energy Development Organization (KEDO), 112
Korean Politics: The Quest for Democratization and Economic Development (Kie-chiang Oh), 55
Korean War (1950–1953), 15, 63, 69, 81
  ended by armistice, 13, 29, 89, 94
    not by treaty, 100
  fiftieth anniversary of, 16, 95
  Kim Il Sung to blame for, 121
  last two years of, 122
  South Korea made garrison state by, 56, 58, 87
  United Nations role in, 119, 120
  U.S. role in, 118
Korea Society Quarterly, 148
Korea Times, 96
Kwangju uprising, 59

Lee Hoi-Chung, 153
Lee Jon Wook, 36
Los Angeles Times (newspaper), 58
Luck, Gary, 114
Luxembourg, 121

MacArthur, Douglas, 13, 90
Maclean's (magazine), 125
Mao Tse–tung, 157, 160
Markle, Kenneth, 91
Médecins sans Frontières (humanitarian relief organization), 163
media, 31, 36, 41, 96
  control of, in North Korea, 77
  news reports from Pyongyang and, 160, 161
  one-sided American reporting in, 32, 33, 66
  embargo on news and, 27
Meretzki, Hans, 75
Middle Eastern oil exports, 132
military coup, 58–59
Military Defense Commission of the Supreme People's Assembly, 65
Military Demarcation Line (MDL), 114
military forces, U.S.
  attack on, in Dhahran, 35
  peace maintained by, in Asia-Pacific region, 139
  in Persian Gulf, 36
  in South Korea, 18, 30, 87, 100, 143
    alleged crimes committed by, 91, 95, 96
    cause of tension, 60, 114
    unnecessary, 90
    withdrawal of, 89
      advocated by increasing numbers of South Koreans, 88, 116
      appropriate, 28, 93, 115, 117–18
      con, 94–97
      Kim Jong Il's desire for, 153
missiles, 143, 162
  flight testing by North Korea, 18, 37, 41, 103
    across Japan, 99, 109, 114, 138
    moratorium on, 23, 117, 148
  North Korean development of, 38, 91
    need for defense program against, 34–37
    need for negotiation against, 39–42
    U.S. provocation of, 29
Mutual Defense Treaty (1953), 29–30

Namkung, Tony, 105
National Assembly (South Korea), 50, 60
National Defense Commission (North Korea), 145
National Security Council (South Korea), 154
National Security Law (South Korea), 53, 153
natural disasters in North Korea, 65–66, 69
New Asia (magazine), 36
New York Times (newspaper), 27, 28
Nobel Peace Prize, 27, 144
Nodong missiles, 23, 99, 138
Nogunri allegations of killings by U.S. troops, 95
North Korea, 12, 13, 15, 103
  closed to outside world, 46, 99
  compared to China, 156, 157–58, 162
  demonization of, 30
  desire to improve relations with U.S., 105, 117
    cynicism about U.S. intentions and, 104
  disadvantages of Korean unification for, 139
  fiftieth anniversary celebrations of, 65
  inspections of nuclear facilities in, 31
  natural disasters in, 66, 69

production of plutonium stopped by, 99, 101
resilience of socialism in, 68–69, 80, 153
Soviet occupation of, 56
successes of, 67–68
threat from, 20–23, 36–37, 100, 153
  continuing nuclear program and, 110
  exaggeration of, 26, 41, 114
  includes weapons of mass destruction, 16, 24, 132, 138
  need for missile defense system against, 34
  provoked by U.S. missiles in South Korea, 29
  increasing as new missiles developed, 38
  light water reactors and, 111
  as logical strategy, 91–92, 130–31
  public declaration of, 109
tight control kept over, 45, 155
see also economy of Korea; foreign policy
Nuclear Non-Proliferation Treaty (NPT), 18, 114, 132
nuclear weapons, 91, 133, 143
  North Korea denies possession of, 24
  North Korean agreement to limit, 98, 99, 101–102, 117
    questionable reliability of, 110, 111
  twelve countries in possession of, 37
  U.S. possession of, in South Korea, 29, 100

Oberdorfer, Don, 12
Oh, Katy, 13
Oh, Susan, 125
Olympic Games (Australia 2000), 125, 147
Orbis, 140

Pacific War, 58
PAC missiles, 36
Pakistan, 99, 109
Park Chung Hee, 45, 58, 59
Parks, Michael, 155
Pasicolan, Paolo, 119
Patriot missiles, 29
Peace Review, 91
peace treaty
  China and U.S. should endorse, 117
  need for, 142–43
  should be with UN, not U.S., 119–22
People's Korea (journal), 31
Perry, William, 111, 141
Persian Gulf War, 34, 35
Persson, Goran, 148

plutonium, 99, 101, 102
political prisoners, 53, 75–76, 81
  defectors and, 82–83
Public Security Ministry (North Korean police), 78
Putin, Vladimir, 41
Pyongyang, 23, 65, 66, 154
  capital of North Korea, 12
  handicapped persons removed from, 82
  need for U.S. embassy in, 142
  need for U.S. liaison office in, 105

al Qaeda terrorist network, 36

refugees, 103, 140
  potential flood of, from North Korea, 21, 100
  Seoul unprepared for, 139
Republic of Korea (ROK). *See* South Korea
reunification, 15, 16, 72, 126, 159
  ambiguities associated with, 154
  economic aspects of, 125, 128–29
  Korean leaders' discussion about, 146
  need for long-term approach to, 137, 144, 148, 149, 158
  North Korean desire for, 20, 21
  security threat would be reduced by, 130–32
  world powers can help achieve peacefully, 127, 134, 135
    need for Seoul to prepare for, 133
  world powers should not push for, 136
    because Korean situation is dangerous, 138
    because of possible effects in Northeast Asia, 139–41
Rhee, Syngman, 57, 58, 62
rogue states
  need to remove North Korea from list of, 30, 105, 142
  North Korea portrayed as, 98, 99, 100
  threats posed by, 35–38
    exaggerations about, 40
Roh Tae Woo, 53, 60
Rumsfeld Commission, 138
Russia, 121, 145, 146
  ally of North Korea, 120
  encouragement of missile reduction in North Korea, 41
  Korean reunification and, 127, 128, 131, 132, 140
  weapon sales to South Korea from, 90

Sae Woom Tuh, 91

Savage, Tim, 41
Scud missiles, 23, 99, 102
  difficulty of shooting down, 36
  used by Saddam Hussein against
    Israel, 35
Senate Armed Services Committee, 34
Senate Foreign Relations Committee,
  111
Seoul, 12, 92, 128, 131, 133
  Kim Jong Il to visit, 147, 154
  possibility of refugees flooding to,
    139
Seoul-Shinuiju railway, 147
September 11 terrorist attacks, 36
Shahab missile, 109
Sha Zukang, 41
Shuja, Sharif M., 103, 116
Sigal, Leon V., 30, 39
social class system of Korea, 20, 56–57,
  75
  autocracy and, 58
  growth of middle class and, 59
socialism, 71
  in North Korea, 67–69, 72, 73, 80,
    153
    economic inefficiency of, 78–79
    see also Juche ideology
South Korea, 12, 19, 51, 143
  American military government in, 56
  capable of own defense, 93
    with large army, 58
  economic success of, 15
  human rights in, 46, 53
  Kim Dae Jung's reforms in, 50, 52,
    54
  lack of missile defense system in, 138
  need for cooperation with North, 92,
    116
  need to improve security in
    Northeast Asia, 24, 41
    threat from North and, 18, 23
  peace the most important goal of,
    145
  reunification and, 134, 139
  transition from military to
    democratic rule, 45, 47
    American prompting and, 56
    peaceful nature of, 48
  UN resolution to protect, 13
  see also democracy; Sunshine Policy
South-North Joint Declaration, 147,
  149
Soviet Union, 15, 45, 90, 148
  aid to Korea ended following break-
    up of, 100
  economic reform in, 161
  North Korean troops trained by, 87
  role in founding North Korea, 12–13

Special Operations Forces (North
  Korean), 23–24
State Department, U.S., 75, 80, 120,
  122, 142
State Security Agency (North Korea),
  78
Status of Forces Agreement (SOFA),
  95, 96, 97
Stephens, Hugh, 64
Struck, Doug, 125
student uprising, 58, 59
Sun-chul Yang, 148
Sung-Chul Choi, 67
Sunoo, Harold, 32–33
Sunshine Policy, 125, 141, 147–48
  courage required for, 150
  divisive in South Korea, 154
  ineffectiveness of, 152–53
  need for reexamination of, 151
  open dialogue with North Korea the
    core of, 144
  peaceful coexistence the goal of, 149
  three principles of, 145
  see also June 2000 summit
Supreme People's Assembly (North
  Korea), 77
Swomley, John M., 26

Taepo Dong missiles, 23, 38, 99, 103,
  138
  launched by North Korea over
    Japan, 37
Taylor, William J., 136
Team Spirit (war exercises), 31
13th World Festival of Youth and
  Students (Pyongyang 1989), 82
Tonghak tradition, the, 56, 57, 58
Trading with the Enemy Act (TWEA),
  106
Treverton, Gregory F., 155
Truman, Harry S., 87, 90
Turkey, 121
20th Century Korea (Sunoo), 33

Understanding Human Rights in North
  Korea (Sung-Chul Choi), 67
United Nations (UN), 12, 13, 29, 30
  Development Program, 106
  Human Rights Subcommittee, 76
  role in Korean War, 119
    as first international military
      intervention, 120, 121
    need for peace treaty between UN
      and North Korea necessitated by,
      122
United Nations Command (UNC),
  115, 118, 122
United Nations Security Council, 120

United States, 12, 13, 143, 145, 158
  Department of Defense, 19, 26
  Korean unification and, 127, 128, 139
  lack of national missile defense
    system in, 138
  obligation to improve defense on
    Korean Peninsula, 24
  reluctance to make peace agreement
    with North Korea, 117
  role in security of Korea, 134
  see also foreign policy; military forces,
    U.S.

Vietnam, 157
Vollertsen, Norbert, 16

Washington Post (newspaper), 121, 126
weapons of mass destruction, 16,
  131–33, 138, 153

  as bargaining power in North Korea,
    115, 130
  need to defend citizens from, 34, 38
  see also missiles; nuclear weapons
Wells, Andrew, 91
Wolfowitz, Paul, 34
Workers' Party (North Korea), 15, 75,
  76, 78, 153
World Bank, 135, 143
World War II, 12, 87
Wortzel, Larry M., 119
Wright, David, 98

Yearn Hong Choi, 58
Yeon Hacheong, 160
Yongbyon, 24, 101
Yoon Geum Yi, 91